A New Puppy in the Family

A New Puppy in the Family

How to choose and care for your new pet

Elaine Everest

howtobooks

Published by How To Books Ltd
Spring Hill House, Spring Hill Road
Begbroke, Oxford OX5 1RX, United Kingdom
Tel: (01865) 375794, Fax: (01865) 370162
info@howtobooks.co.uk
www.howtobooks.co.uk

How To Books greatly reduce the carbon footprint of their
books by sourcing their typesetting and printing in the UK.

British Library Cataloguing in Publication Data
A catalogue record for this book is available from the British Library

ISBN 978 1 84528 452 7

Illustrations by David Mostyn
Cover design by Omnipress
Produced for How To Books by Deer Park Productions, Tavistock
Typeset by Kestrel Data, Exeter, Devon
Printed and bound in Great Britain by Bell & Bain Ltd, Glasgow

NOTE: The material contained in this book is set out in good faith for
general guidance and no liability can be accepted for loss or expense
incurred as a result of relying in particular circumstances on statements
made in the book. Laws and regulations are complex and liable to change,
and readers should check the current position with the relevant authorities
before making personal arrangements.

To all the Paddipaws dogs and the many lovely people who have owned them or still do. Thank you for loving our babies and giving them such good homes.

Remembering: Sabastian, Holly, Dotti, Ziggy, Oliver, Hayley, Oscar, Peggy, Gracie, William, Chuckie and Nelson.

My three oldies still here to cuddle, Buster, Squidgey and Molly.

Contents

Introduction

Owning a dog does enrich one's life. Dogs are faithful friends and never judge you, whatever you have done. All they request in return is a warm bed, food in their stomachs and a friend to pat them on the head.

For many of us life is marked by our dogs – first as puppies, then the fun-filled years and finally saying goodbye. They are in our care for such a short time that we must make the most of those years lest we live in regret.

This book is for anyone thinking of purchasing a puppy and for those who are the lucky owners of their first dogs.

This is not a user manual on how to run your dog from cradle to grave but a book full of tips and points on where to go for help and answers when looking for a puppy or caring for a dog. It is written using knowledge gained over nearly 40 years of dog breeding and ownership.

Think carefully before choosing a puppy – they are not fashion statements and should not be used for one-upmanship to be better than your neighbours or your family. A dog is for life, whether it be your life or theirs. This can be as long as 20 years with some breeds, or just a few if the dog is taken too early.

My dogs have kept me poor but I wouldn't change one moment of my life spent with them. They've helped me through illness and bereavement and other sad times. They have been there as my friends, in fact they are my family and have never deserted me. You cannot say that of many humans.

I have referred to your puppy as 'he' throughout this book – though of course all the advice still applies if you have a 'she'!

Make the most of your dog while he is with you or you will have just memories to keep you warm.

Elaine Everest is the author of *Showing Your Dog: A Beginner's Guide* and *Canine Cuisine* (How To Books).

1

Finding the Best Puppy for You

SHOPPING FOR A DOG

I use the word 'shopping' as this is really what you are doing when purchasing a puppy. Very much as we would make certain considerations when buying a second-hand car we must make decisions about purchasing our puppy. A dog will be with the family a lot longer than a car, so why when purchasing a puppy do so many people make snap decisions that they will live to regret for many years to come, but deliberate over a vehicle that will have a much shorter life?

WHERE TO SEE DOGS

Even if you have no interest in dog shows these are the places where a variety of dogs can be seen. You will also be able to speak to breeders and owners of the dogs and be able to have a cuddle of the dogs when given permission.

♦ Discover Dogs, held each November in London, gives those people interested in dogs the chance to see an example of every breed of pedigree dog.

♦ Crufts, held over four days at the National Exhibition Centre in Birmingham, has the cream of the canine world on show, as well as the popular Discover Dogs section, making it possible to see every type of breed each day of the show. It's a great place to shop for your dog as well!

♦ Apart from these big events there are dog shows every week of the year where you can watch dogs and ask lots of questions. Publications such as the weekly *Our Dogs* canine newspaper list dog shows as well as interesting news about dogs in general.

WHAT KIND OF DOG FOR ME?

Big, small or giant breeds? Lazy breeds, lively breeds or those somewhere in between? Smooth coats, long coats and even curly coats or hairless? The choice of which dog will live with your family is a very big consideration. Think of the following points when choosing your kind of dog:

♦ Do I have the time to take a dog for a long walk every day, perhaps even twice?

♦ Can I afford the food bills and other costs for a giant breed?

♦ Do I have time to groom a long-coated dog or learn how to clip a terrier with definite style needs?

- Can I afford a groomer if I cannot groom my own dog?

- Do I have a garden that can accommodate a dog?

- Am I house-proud or does slobber and a shedding coat not bother me?

- Do I mind never wearing black again as it shows up every dog hair?

- Do I want a dog that will sit on my lap or one to lie at my feet?

- Do I have lots of stairs on my property that may be a problem to very small or elderly dogs?

- Will my landlord let me keep a dog in the home I rent?

- Will my neighbours be upset by a dog that barks loudly?

Buying a dog is not as easy as you once thought is it? Even choosing the shape and size of a dog can take some time before you even start to visit a breeder.

I've owned dogs in the past but still made sure that I found out a lot about the breed by speaking to people who have owned Yorkshire Terriers. I also read lots of books on the breed.

Dawn Hudd

Pedigree or cross breed?
What is your choice? It is after all a personal choice of which type of dog will live comfortably in your home. Please do not listen

to those people who declare that a cross-breed, a mongrel or a 'Heinz 57', as dogs of indeterminable breeding have been named over the years, are healthier than pedigree dogs. All dogs can be sickly and all dogs can be healthy. Just as some human families seem to be healthier than others so are dogs bred from some parents. Do your homework correctly and you will go some way to making sure that your puppy comes from healthy stock. I know that I would rather purchase a puppy from health-checked parents than take a chance on a mongrel with unknown parentage.

Designer dogs

So what is a designer dog? It is a name that seems to have entered our vocabulary of late and is linked to all things celebrity and shallow. Many people have jumped on to the bandwagon and are advertising dogs with such names as a cockapoo (a cocker spaniel crossed with a poodle), a Pomchi (a cross between a Pomeranian and a Chihuahua) or even a Golden Oldie (a golden retriever crossed with an Old English Sheepdog). Can you see the common word here? Yes, it is crossed – these dogs are all cross-breeds but still those breeding them are charging prices higher than you would pay for the purebred version of each part of the cross. Some people will tell you that these dogs have been bred to share the better points of each breed, to breed out possible health-related problems, but until many generations have been bred and studied can anyone say that they have designed a new health-perfect breed? This includes probably the most well-known new breed – the Labradoodle. It is a cross-breed and not a recognised breed. You don't believe me? Go check out the websites that show specimens of this so called 'breed', and you will see that the dogs come in all shapes and sizes. Any purebred dog has a recognised size range plus other conformation guidelines (which are called a breed standard). At the moment the Labradoodle does not have a standard, or if it does no dogs seem to conform to one. One day there may be a recognised standard, but until then it is just another cross-breed dog.

I'm sorry to have to point this out, especially if you have paid out large sums of money, but if you have one of these so-called designer dogs you have money to waste on a name only and your dog is not a named purebred dog just a cross-breed or a mongrel.

Unsure if this is a breed?

Go to the excellent website belonging to the UK Kennel Club. You will find a list of every type of breed registered in the UK. If the breed of puppy in the advert is not listed as a recognised breed by the Kennel Club please DON'T BUY IT!

Each breed registered with the Kennel Club will have at least one recognised club associated to the type of dog you are interested in. With links to these breed clubs and a band of people ready to answer your questions, purchasing a puppy is easy – if you know where to look.

BUYING A PUPPY

Would you buy your puppy from an advert in a newsagent's window?

Sadly we often spot adverts in newsagent's windows where breeders, and I use the term loosely, offer little puppies for sale. Usually there are spelling mistakes in the breed name and contact is by mobile telephone. There is never a reference to any health testing on the parents or whether they are registered with the Kennel Club. There is always a price that ends with several zeros. Avoid these adverts at all costs. No breeder in their right mind sells a puppy by advertising it on the back of a postcard or an old envelope.

Would you buy your puppy from the internet?
My answer to this would be that it depends upon the website. Avoid at all costs any website that takes adverts from all and sundry, mixing made-up breeds along with known names. Be very wary of any advert that uses words such as, 'teacup', olde worlde' or the word, 'cross' when you are looking for a purebred dog. Any change to a recognised Kennel Club registered breed should make alarm bells ring at once.

There seems to be a fringe group of people who try to dupe unsuspecting buyers of pedigree dogs by making up names of breeds and charging the earth for them. I like to think of these people as the Arthur Daleys of the dog breeding world. 'Hello, mate, wanna buy a dodgy dog? One careful owner.' No thank you!

Would you buy your puppy from a neighbour?
That depends on the neighbour and his dogs! If your neighbour breeds dogs and knows all about the health history of his dogs and is a good owner then why not? Your breeder will be at hand to advise you throughout the dog's life and also there to take him back if circumstances dictate you are no longer able to keep the dog.

Where can you find a dog?

My first port of call would be the Kennel Club to find a puppy list. Their website gives a complete list of every registered breed. Click on the list for the breed for which you want to see the names of the people who have registered their litters of puppies with the Kennel Club and who still have puppies available for sale.

When you click on your chosen breed you will see a map of the UK. Do not home in on your own area but open up the complete list. Be prepared to travel to find a well-bred puppy. You next need to know who on this list are reputable breeders. Sadly some of these people will not know the breed well and unless you are part of that breed's community you could still find yourself with a badly-bred dog.

Armed with the names and details of the breeders sit down with your telephone and ring each one. You need to know the answers to the following questions:

- How long has the person been in the breed? Some people buy a bitch and breed for money.

- Do they belong to any breed clubs? A responsible breeder will be part of the canine world.

- Do they show their dogs/or do they take an active part in the breed community?

- Do they own the mother? Some people buy in puppies to sell.

- How many litters has the mother had? Some people over-breed a bitch for the money.

♦ Are the breeder's dogs good with children? You only have their word for this, a visit will show more.

♦ Do they have documented proof that the dam and sire (mother and father) have gone through any health checks required for that breed? You can find the list in a later part of this book, on page 21.)

♦ When are the puppies available to leave their mother? A pertinent question if it is near to Christmas – some people breed for the gift market! Good breeders hold on to puppies and do not let them go over the holidays or if they are under eight to ten weeks depending on the size of the breed.

♦ The price? It's always good to know what people charge but don't be swayed by cut prices.

At this point you will have whittled down your list as some puppies will have been sold, or you may not have liked the person you spoke to (it is often a good idea to trust your own gut feeling) or you are not happy with their answers. Do not make an appointment to view the puppies yet as you will be swayed by the cuteness of the litter.

Next, telephone the breed club secretary for your breed. There may be more than one depending on the number of clubs for the breed. Again the Kennel Club will show a list of breed clubs for each breed. No one is going to tell you that someone is a rubbish breeder; they do not want to be sued. However, you can ask if the people on the list are known to them and who, if they were purchasing a puppy, they would buy from of those names. The breed club secretary may also be able to tell you of any other breeders who have puppies.

Some breed clubs have a website and do have a puppy co-ordinator who can put you in touch with known breeders, or even an older dog needing a new home. Never underestimate a breed club, they are there to help every owner of that breed and are worth their weight in gold.

Your list of prospective litters should now be looking good and you are ready to make an appointment to visit them.

I looked at various breeds of dog and their temperaments online and spoke to friends who have Cavalier King Charles Spaniels. I read the club websites so that I was aware of health issues within the breed. Once I had decided that this was the breed for us I started looking for a puppy. Luckily a friend knew of a litter and when their background was checked everything was OK.

Sarah Alpe

BUYING A PUPPY FROM A RESCUE CENTRE

National rescue centres each have their own procedures for seeking puppies. My personal thoughts are that if you want a pedigree puppy then go to the expert breeder as the history of the dog is known, and in my mind that is important, especially if the dog is being introduced into a home with a young family.

Our last family dog was a rescue Staffie called Jess who was the successor to our gundogs and my cocker rescued from the NCDL. Whilst completely different in every way Jess won my heart over as one of the most intuitive dogs, a quality I believe bull breeds possess in droves. With this, coupled with an enormous personality and mind of their own, comic spirit and boundless energy, they are perfect. Plus Molly is small for a Miniature Bull Terrier these days and as such is a great compact size!

Anna Webb

Ask about the puppy's history, as it may be that the mother was taken into the centre before she gave birth. Try to find out the mother's history, as sometimes it is known if the dog was handed in whilst in whelp.

If buying a dog from a rescue centre is a cost saving exercise for the family it is worth sitting down with pen and paper and making a list of the ongoing expense of owning that dog once he comes to live with you. Food, insurance and day-to-day care as well as time spent caring and exercising the animal can add up considerably. Buying a cheap dog does not always equate to a saving.

We just liked the look of Hank, a Lurcher/Airedale cross, when we walked into the RSPCA rescue centre (he was sitting behind the counter with the receptionist). When we got Eric we knew we liked the terrier in Hank and had done some research on the terrier breed.

Hazel Davis

Home checks

Home checks are usually undertaken by rescue centres who want to know a little about the family home before handing over a puppy or fully grown dog.

Usually the person inspecting your home will check your garden to see if it is 'dog friendly' and also ask about who is at home to take care of the dog. You will be questioned about your children, their ages and whether they have had experience of living with a dog. You will often find that if you have a desired breed or type of dog you are gently persuaded to think of other breeds, breeds that they have a high stock of in the centre. Stick to your guns and do not be persuaded to consider a breed that you are not keen on. In fact if you have your heart set on a certain type of breed contact breed rescue (through the breed club) rather than a general rescue society as they are more experienced with that particular type of dog. They can tell you so much more about the breed and will have experience of how to train and live with the breed.

When purchasing a purebred dog from a breeder it is unlikely that you will have to go through a home check. However, they will want to know a lot about you before they hand over that carefully bred and nurtured little puppy. Do not expect to turn up at a breeder's home and leave ten minutes later with a puppy after handing over a wad of £20 notes. It may be that you have to visit several times before the puppy can be taken to his new home. If you have children the breeder will want to meet them and observe them with their other dogs. Come to that, you and your spouse will also be observed to make sure you are happy with a dog running around your feet, climbing on your lap and possibly spraying you with water after an enjoyable drink.

I have a fond memory of a gentleman arriving to see my puppies. For some reason I didn't take to him and thought I'd put him through the 'Oliver Test'. If he survived then I would contemplate allowing him to purchase one of my little brood. Oliver, the father of the puppies, walked into the room. He was in full coat and looked every ounce of his seven stone weight. Oliver walked up to the man and rubbed his head up the side of the man's leg before gently climbing onto his lap and laying one heavy paw on his shoulder before delivering a large sloppy kiss on the man's face. I waited with bated breath for him to shy away or run from the room (not that he could, weighed down as he was by Oliver). In fact the man beamed and hugged the dog declaring he had been worried that we would not let him have one of our puppies as he had not owned a dog for several years. It seemed he had grown up with Old English Sheepdogs and had dreamed of the day he would have his own home and could show his own children what a special breed they were. In time two of our puppies went to live with him and were much loved and very welcomed additions to the family.

The home visit started with an inspection of the garden, as she was keen to ensure it was secured with full fencing. Then she came in and asked how old the children were, whether other children visited the house, who was at home, how long the house was left empty, etc. She asked what sort of dog we wanted, and suggested that a pup was a better option. The rest was a general chat really about the reasons we wanted a dog, what dog experience we had. Fairly informal but I think she gathered all the info she needed.

Catherine Burrows

RESPONSIBILITIES

A breeder's responsibility

What should the breeder supply to their puppy buyers? What should you expect from the breeder? Come to that, what should they be doing to show to the buyer that they are thinking of the puppy when they breed?

Yes, you should definitely receive your healthy puppy but what else should the breeder supply you with? Would you leave a maternity ward with a new-born baby without instructions on care from the midwife or healthcare worker? It is the same with a puppy. The person who brought it into the world and has known this little scrap for the past eight to ten weeks should hand over information that will make his transition into adulthood with your family trouble free. Further on in this chapter I show the list of items that are usually provided by a breeder (see page 20), but there are things more important than material items that a good breeder should supply.

♦ You should feel from your first visit that the breeder loves their dogs and does not see them as just a money-making machine. They should have been involved with the breed for some time before breeding and be members of the breed community. How can they help you if they are not part of the breed themselves?

♦ You need to feel confident that the breeder has the care of their particular breed in mind when breeding. Not just health but the continuation of the bloodlines for that

breed and breeding to the standard laid down by the
Kennel Club. In fact it is a good idea to download a copy
of your chosen breed's standard and take it with you on
your first visit. Ask the breeder to go through it with you
showing you the points of the dog on the mother and any
other dogs he or she may have. This will show whether
they are aware of their breed and what is important about
the construction of the dog for it to have a healthy and
happy future.

♦ Check that the breeder has membership as a Kennel Club
accredited breeder. I would like to know that the breeder
belongs to this scheme but it is not paramount on my list of
requirements. I support the Kennel Club but as yet there are
too many loopholes for backyard breeders to join the scheme
and tag the Accredited Breeder title to their selling scams.

♦ A good breeder will not allow visitors to see the puppies, let
alone handle them, until they are old enough to stand and
feed unaided. This is usually around four to five weeks of age.
Cross infection is a big worry and no breeder wants visitors
to walk anything into the home that would harm the little
dogs. Furthermore, the mother of the puppies will not want
her little brood manhandled until they are not so reliant on
her. Even the most even-tempered bitches can be snappy if
strangers approach their babies. This is nature and not a sign
of an aggressive dog.

I send out a questionnaire as the first stage and those really interested will send it back to me. Then it's a phone conversation, a visit to meet our dogs and have a more in-depth chat and then if I'm happy with everything I'll put them on the waiting list for a puppy. I also look up their address on Google earth so I can see where they live, this also helps you to know if you're getting the full picture from them!

Terrie Cousins-Brown

The dog owner's responsibility

The owner too must show that they will be responsible for the dog for the rest of his life. With some dogs this is in excess of 15 years. It may be worth considering where you expect your life to be in 15 years' time and will your dog be part of this life? If this poses a problem with your life plans then perhaps reconsider whether owning a dog is really top of your priorities.

The least you can do for the breeder of your dog is to keep in touch and update them on the puppy's progress. If you move home let them know so that they can keep in touch. Over the years I've received some lovely photographs of my 'babies' and marvelled at the lovely dogs they have turned into. I've also shared sad news and can still shed a tear for the loss of little Rosie who died in a house fire despite the frantic work of the fire service to resuscitate her. She was much loved and will always be missed by her doting owners.

When visiting a breeder you are selling yourself and your family to them. You need to assure them that you and your family are able to care for a dog and that he will fit into your family's life as soon as he arrives home.

Having a young child I needed to be sure I was choosing a breed which would be happy in a loud, hectic, busy family environment, and who would be playful but tolerant of children and visitors.

I keep in touch with Matilda's breeder. She asked for updates on the puppy's progress as often as I could oblige. I have been sending her lots of photos and snippets of news. More importantly, she asked to keep in touch in case we ever needed to rehome our pup. She said she would always have a home for her.

Kelly Rose Bradford

Sadly more dogs are abandoned, handed back to breeders or handed into rescue centres due to them not fitting into a family of young children. Reports that they bite are sometimes down to the child. To be honest I've felt like biting a child when its incessant shrieking is left uncontrolled so can sympathise with any puppy that retaliates. I prefer not to sell a puppy to any family with very young children but many breeders do.

If you have young children in your family you need to consider if they are old enough to live with a dog. Children under five can be very demanding and have to learn that the family dog needs its own space. Dogs do not always want to be manhandled and played with but need time to sleep and eat. When they are teething they can have teeth as sharp as needles, they will chew toys and jump up to play. Many breeds of dogs are large enough to be a hazard around toddlers. Without any bad temperament a dog can still trip up a toddler or knock her over. The parents will need eyes in the back of their heads at all times when the pair are together. At no time should the dog and child be left alone. Whoever is to blame, and it is not always the dog's fault, it is too late to point a finger when a child has been injured through a parent's neglect or ill judgement.

Can you cope with a young dog and a young child? Can you train both to live with each other? If you have any doubts, wait until the child is older before introducing a puppy into the family.

Babies

If you are planning to start a family, will the dog still be a big part of your lives or will he be shunned in favour of the new arrival when she is born? The dog will be puzzled why one moment he was your favourite companion only to be shut away when a strange little being arrives. In some families babies and dogs do not mix so ask yourself if you are prepared to accept a dog into a home where he will not be as popular when a baby arrives. A dog is not a short-term replacement for a baby until a couple can afford the real thing. He will be with you for many years and you must account for his needs as well as the needs of any family that come along after his arrival.

COLLECTING YOUR PUPPY

If you thought that collecting a tiny puppy would mean leaving the breeder's home with just a squirming puppy tucked under your arm you are wrong. It is quite normal to leave with a pile of paperwork and canine paraphernalia. Some of the documents are legal and are a very important part of owning a healthy happy puppy. The remaining items are to help you start out without worry so you can enjoy living with your puppy from day one of your lives together.

The breeder will want to go through the paperwork with you so never expect just to collect the puppy and leave. Even at the point of departure a breeder can change their mind about selling a puppy to you if they feel that you are not taking their advice seriously. In fact after a puppy has gone to its new home if the breeder hears that the little dog is not being cared for properly it has been known for a breeder to take back the dog. I know of one breeder who found out a puppy she had sold was not being cared for. She went to the home and took back the dog which lived the rest of his life out with the breeder. Breeders keep the welfare of every dog they breed as their number one priority. To them breeding is not about the money.

Here is a list of what to expect to receive from your puppy breeder and why it is needed.

♦ A diet sheet showing what your puppy is eating at the moment and the regularity of the meals. This sheet should also show at what age to change meals. The breeder should also go through the feeding routine with you.

♦ Photographs of both parents along with contact details of the sire of the puppy.

♦ A copy of the puppy's pedigree. This is the family history of the puppy and can be very interesting. Books about the breed may well hold information about your puppy's ancestors as well as photographs. Tracing your puppy's family history can be as interesting as searching for your own ancestors and with pedigree dogs can be well documented. When the breeder first shows you the pedigree a number of champions may be pointed out to you. Take note that if these come from the father's side of the pedigree it may be that the breeder simply paid for the use of the dog at stud. Some stud dog owners let their dogs mate with many bitches, not all of them are good examples of the breed. The breeder will have an affix/kennel name. This is a name that is registered with the Kennel Club and has been granted to the breeder to add to the front of every one of their puppies' registered names. If they bought a dog in it is added at the end of the name. Any decent breeder will have an affix.

♦ Copies of all health screenings that are relevant to the breed undertaken for each of the parents. Ideally these should be given to you when you make your first visit to the breeder so you have time to check out the details. If your puppy is a cross-breed (and that includes so-called designer dogs) there should still be health screening/tests undertaken on any of the puppy's parents that the owner professes to be of pure breeding. If the documents are photocopied contact the vet, Kennel Club or testing organisation to confirm that the documents are correct and have not been tampered with.

♦ Kennel Club registration documents. If these are not ready then withhold part of the payment until the paperwork is delivered to you. Remember also to sign and return the documents to the Kennel Club registration department so that your own name can be added to the papers.

♦ Insurance cover. This cover will run for up to six weeks and give you peace of mind until you take out a pet care policy for your puppy. Your breeder will register your puppy and you will receive information from the insurer but it is your choice to shop around to find the best policy for your puppy.

♦ Samples of all the food being fed to your puppy. Whether your puppy is on a well-known brand of puppy food or on a more sensible puppy diet your breeder should pack up enough food to see you through the next three days. Ideally you will have seen the diet sheet and prepared for puppy's home coming but this pack will ensure that you are covered while you stock up.

♦ A piece of bedding. You may laugh at this as you will most likely have purchased a bed and lots of washable fleece but this piece of blanket is very important and is something that all good breeders supply. The night before your puppy leaves the comfort and safety of sleeping with its siblings and mother the breeder will place the bedding into the sleeping area where it will pick up the familiar scent of the family. Yes the bedding will be stained and slightly smelly but this will be your puppy's comfort blanket while he settles into his new life.

♦ Receipt of purchase. This is not just a piece of paper that states you have handed over many hundreds of pounds. It is proof that the dog is legally yours from the date on the paperwork.

♦ Contract. Your breeder should give some sort of contract that will show that they have bred with care and that they are there to help you throughout all the days of your dog's life. Furthermore they are available to hold your hand through any problem you may have with your dog and that if circumstances dictate you are no longer able to keep your dog they will either take back the dog or if that is not possible they will find a good home for your pet and continue to watch over him for the rest of that dog's life.

♦ Vaccination paperwork. The timing for a puppy's first inoculations can differ from vet to vet. The first can be given at the age of eight weeks with the next following two weeks later. Quite often the puppy will leave for his new home before the course has been completed. If the new home is far away it may be impossible to travel back for that second shot. Therefore, a detailed certificate of what has been given to your puppy is required along with batch numbers of the drugs just in case there is a problem at a later date.

♦ Worming certificate. Your puppy will have been wormed several times before he leaves for his new home. Your breeder will give you a certificate showing when puppy had his doses and which brand of medication was given. If you are unsure of when your puppy should next be wormed then ask your breeder rather than follow directions on the back of a box. If your puppy hasn't been wormed before he leaves the breeder don't be dismayed to find small worms in his stools when you administer the medication. It is natural for all puppies to have a few worms when they are born. However, if left untreated, intestinal worms will leave a puppy in poor condition and could cause slower growth and general poor health.

♦ Information on books and other literature as well as websites and blogs about dog care and the breed of the dog.

♦ Details of puppy socialisation classes, general training classes and also showing, obedience or other canine hobby training that you may wish to pursue with your family.

♦ Breed club details. For owners of purebred dogs it is fun to keep in touch with other owners of your chosen breed and joining a breed club is the way to do this. Apart from newsletters and dog shows, good clubs arrange pet events where you can learn about grooming, training and just having fun with your dog.

♦ Fun things. Toys, photographs of his life so far and bowls, dishes and chews are quite often given by the breeder who will miss this little scrap that has been part of their life for the past few months. Don't be surprised if there are tears when the breeder waves goodbye to your puppy!

Much of the paperwork will be in a folder, although some breeders write their own booklets for the puppy owner. However it is supplied, take time when you arrive home to go through the documents and deal with any that need sending to the Kennel Club or insurance company. I do cover insurance choices in another part of this book but usually you are covered for a few weeks so you will have time to investigate all options rather than taking out an annual policy with the company which has supplied your free cover.

I would expect to get a puppy history and health records from the breeder. I'd like to know their likes and dislikes, full worming treatment details and a supply of food that they had been on to ensure consistency of diet. Probably one of the most important things is to be able to contact them with any questions or advice that's needed in the early days.

Sarah Alpe

KEEPING IN TOUCH WITH THE BREEDER

The breeder of your puppy will be there for the length of the puppy's life. In fact you will probably be in touch for a long time after your dog has gone to the Rainbow Bridge after enjoying a happy and long life. The dog world is a close community and owning a dog makes you part of a community that will be a part of your life forever.

Never be afraid to pick up the telephone and let the breeder know of any worry or indeed any high points in the puppy's life. They want to know how he or she is growing and a photograph of the little dog from time to time will be treasured.

For anyone hoping to exhibit their dog or compete with it in other canine activities the breeder will be there every step of the way as you prepare for your new hobby.

Many breeders now have their information in booklet form which is a help to the new owner. With breeders owning websites there is no reason for the purchaser ever to lose touch with the person who bred their puppy.

I keep in touch with all my puppy owners. I have a spreadsheet with details of every litter and the owners. I tend to email out anything of interest to them and send greetings at Christmas. I also send them details of club events.

Terrie Cousins-Brown

The author's thoughts

My personal wish is that it should be illegal to sell puppies via adverts in newsagents' windows, in the free adverts and on websites set up by non-qualified people. Ideally the RSPCA should be the people to police these types of sales and stop puppy breeding by the wrong type of person – those who are doing it only for the money. I would also like to see this organisation and others like it working more closely with The Kennel Club rather than taking any opportunity to point the finger at the people who breed pedigree dogs.

Anyone contemplating breeding a litter of puppies should be prepared to turn down a purchaser if they do not consider them a suitable person to own one of their puppies. They should also be prepared to take back a dog they have bred, or at the very least help rehome the dog if the owner is no longer able to care for him. No breeder should see the puppies they have so carefully bred end up in a rescue centre.

2

Your home and your puppy

Purchasing a puppy and taking him home may sound very simple but there are many things to consider before your home is even a safe place for the puppy to live. Furniture and everyday fixtures and fittings can be killers to a small animal that has no conception that nibbling a cable or touching something has the potential to kill or seriously harm them. As the new owner of a puppy it is your duty to puppy proof your home and be aware of not only the damage a small puppy can do to the home but what dangers lurk for an inquisitive youngster.

THE HOME

Walk through every room and hallway in your home. Try to adopt the mindset of a small dog and check whether your home is safe for a little dog or could he damage himself or your property?

♦ Are there any exposed cables that could be tugged at or chewed? Have them securely attached to the skirting board or wall, or hidden from view completely.

♦ Block off access to the backs of television sets, hi-fi, washing machines and other electrical equipment that a puppy could sneak behind to get up to mischief. It is not just that they can chew the cables, they will try to tug at hanging leads with the result that the puppy and the item could be damaged if the heavy objects come tumbling down.

♦ Remote controls, mobile phones and any other portable devices will go missing if left on the arm of the sofa or laid on the floor. They are expensive to replace and can do serious damage to a young dog's internal organs if chewed.

♦ The wooden legs of tables and chairs are very enticing to a teething puppy so either move the furniture to another room where the puppy is not allowed or lag the legs with hessian or any other strong fabric that may stop sharp teeth chewing the wood. There are products that can be purchased from a pet shop and dabbed onto chewable surfaces, which will then give off a bitter taste. By taking precautions to protect or move property from his reach and by gradually training him to understand that he is not allowed to chew whatever he chooses your home will soon be safe from little jaws.

♦ Children's toys are very interesting to a young puppy and there will be tears if the puppy eats a favourite doll or a vital part of a game. Children must learn to keep their toys away from the puppy and not encourage the new family member to play with their valued possessions. It is surprising what a puppy will manage to swallow. Sometimes an object appears from the other end of the dog but most items that are swallowed need an expensive and painful operation on the little chap to relieve him of a blockage that could end his short life.

♦ The kitchen or utility room is quite often the place where a puppy will sleep. Even here there are places where the puppy can chew or find interesting items to damage. Add childproof locks to cupboards, especially those holding household detergents. The fridge is also an enticing place as food can miraculously appear and dogs soon learn where the food lives! Wash-baskets and the open door of a washing machine or tumble dryer will reveal socks and underwear than can be swallowed and become lodged in the stomach.

♦ Bathrooms and bedrooms contain toiletries and drugs that can kill a dog. Keep the items high and out of reach or keep the puppy from the room.

♦ Rugs and carpets, however flat and seemingly unattractive to a dog can suddenly be ruined overnight. Urine, faeces and sick can stain the floor coverings or they could just be chewed along with drapes and other furnishings. It is more sensible to contain a puppy somewhere safe than be making claims on your home insurance before the new member of your family has spent one week under your roof.

Dog gates

Sometimes simply closing a door does not keep a dog from entering a room where he is not welcome. Humans forget to close doors and some dogs can learn to push them open. A dog gate is a much better prospect. Any family that has toddlers will confirm that these gates are a godsend. A puppy can sit on one side of a gate and still see his family. Left behind a solid door he will cry and scratch until he is upset, the family are upset and the paintwork on the door has been gouged with tiny claws.

Dog gates are higher than baby gates and are ideal for puppies that are going to grow into tall dogs. If you have a smaller breed then child gates are adequate. Check the gaps between the bars of the gate to make sure that while small the puppy will not wriggle through or become stuck. The gate should also fit securely so as not to be knocked out of the door frame by a boisterous animal, and the opening latch should be secure but easily managed for the humans who need to go back and forth through the opening.

Flooring

Keep floor covering to a minimum while training a puppy. You need a surface that can be wiped over to remove little accidents but not become so slippery that the puppy cannot walk on it. A room with access to the back garden is ideal for him to live in as he can eat and then go outside to do his toilet training. Newspaper left near the door will catch any accidents that happen if you cannot reach the door in time to let him out.

Some people worry about doggy smells in the home, but it is best to avoid spraying air fresheners around the room where the puppy lives as this may make him ill. Strong disinfectant will make the home smell like a public convenience so it is wise to find a fragrance that will smell pleasant and not make a visitor's eyes water. There is a list of recommended products near the end of this book which includes suitable cleaning fluid.

A tip
A squirt of any well-known biological clothes washing liquid in four pints of warm water will wash a floor and remove any urine odour. My own favourite is lavender-scented which leaves a room smelling sweet and 'normal'.

THE GARDEN

Your puppy should know that the garden is a nice place to be and that this is where he has to do his toilet after eating his dinner. The garden can be a dangerous place and again must be puppy proof. If possible, fence off an area so that he cannot stray onto the lawn and dig holes and leave his own deposits. It is fine to have supervised playtime with you in the forbidden area but for the puppy's safety and so that you can clean up after him with ease he needs his own area. Plant pots containing bulbs and flowers can be attractive to a little dog but many bulbs will make him sick if dug up and eaten. You can find a list of dangerous foods and garden items in Chapter 7.

My garden is supposedly dog proof. Titch is never taken for a walk except on a lead. I use the same precautions in the house as I used to use when our children were small, e.g. no trailing electrical leads, no medicines left out, etc., etc . . .

Anthony Milton

WHERE TO SLEEP

A puppy needs to know where he is supposed to sleep. This area will also be his refuge where he can go to rest and have some 'me' time. This is vital in a busy household especially one that has young children running around. This area can also be where he is sent if he has been naughty. It should be the puppy equivalent of 'the naughty step'.

Bedding should be washable and there should be plenty of it. Fleece is the preferred bedding as it can be washed at high temperature and dried within minutes in a tumble dryer or on the washing line. What is so good about fleece bedding for dogs is that any liquid goes through to the lining of the fleece and the fluffier fleece topping stays dry. Puppy will stay dry even if he wets his bedding early in the night. A layer of newspaper underneath the bedding protects the floor of his bed area.

The best item I've ever bought was an Equafleece dog jumper, it is simply the most useful product. Molly hates walking in the rain, and this fleece is 100 per cent water repellent so she stays dry as a bone. Plus being a short single-coated breed, the fleece gives Molly an extra layer of warmth. The florescent yellow one keeps her safe and seen on dark winter mornings and evenings.

Anna Webb

Dog beds

There are many brands of dog beds on the market ranging from the reliable rubber beds that can be scrubbed clean to fancy four posters for tiny toy dogs. The choice is down to you as the owner and what you can afford but most importantly what is best for the type of dog you own.

Dog crates

A very popular item for a dog owner is the dog crate, or cage as it is also known. The crate is not to be used as a prison where a dog is left for hours on end while the owner goes off to work. The crate is a refuge, where a puppy can be fed in private away from other family members or pets and where he can sleep.

When purchasing a crate for your dog you must buy one that is suitable for the adult size of the breed and not a little puppy. The dog should be able to lie down and stretch out his legs. He should also be able to stand up and turn around in comfort. You can see that the size of crate can differ wildly depending on whether you own a West Highland White Terrier or a Great Dane.

Well-made crates will have several doors set either in each end or along the wider side. The top can be hinged so that it can be lifted and the dog removed that way rather than through a door – ideal for a puppy.

There should also be a removable tray that can be slid out and washed, so ideally it should be made of a durable material as it has to cope with a lively dog and withstand much wear and tear.

The whole cage will be collapsible so that it can be moved with ease. Some sizes of cage can also be used in the car, making them a very useful and adaptable piece of equipment for any dog owner.

Crate training

Some puppies will not be happy if put into a strange crate on their first evening at home and left in the dark and alone for the first time in their young lives. Inform your puppy's breeder that you intend to crate train as they may be able to start this while the puppy is still with his littermates so that the large metal cage is not strange to him when he arrives in his new forever home.

Feeding the puppy in his crate and leaving toys scattered in the crate will show that this strange place is not frightening and is his territory. Leaving the door open during the day will allow him to go in and out at all times and not worry unduly when the time comes for you to close the door.

Gradually close the door on him when he is sleeping and reward him with a tiny morsel of food when he has not cried to be let out. Gradually extend the time he is left inside the cage until he is happy to sleep the night through with the door closed.

To begin with you may find that you or another family member will have to sleep downstairs with the puppy until he is happy to sleep the night through. This is not to be thought of as play time. Puppy should be put into his cage, the lights lowered and the television turned off. Yes, puppy may cry during the night but try to resist the urge to pick him up and have a cuddle or you will be working to his agenda and not your own. By all means lift him out if he is restless and you feel he needs to go into the garden for a wee but praise him if he does perform and then place him back into his bed.

Keep the cage within sight of the family during the daytime, even if it is not in its intended home. It can be gradually moved when the puppy has accepted his new bed. Scatter the fleece bedding around the floor close to the bed so that he knows he can sleep on the bedding and it becomes familiar to him. This is the time when you should be building the puppy's confidence so that he accepts his new surroundings and trusts you as his new parent.

TOILET TRAINING

Do not expect your puppy to arrive toilet trained. This is something you must do for yourself. Your breeder should let you know how good your puppy is and how much training he has had to toilet in the right place.

All dogs want to go to the toilet as soon as they have eaten something. From day one start a routine whereby puppy is placed out in the garden as soon as he has been fed. Do not play with him, do not let him sleep but pick him up and go out with him. This is not playtime so just keep repeating your chosen keyword (I use 'wee wee' but you may prefer another word) and let him wander until he has finished.

Praise him at once and then return inside. Gradually he will learn he has been good and that you are pleased with his performance. Your keyword added to your pleasure and praise will soon link the mealtime and the garden with his toilet training.

Until puppy has got the hang of where he goes to the toilet, feed him as near to the back door as possible. If you are crate training have the crate near the door so he can eat in the crate and then go outside. He will feel comfortable eating in the crate and if the door is kept open he will learn to walk outside to do his business.

Keep a bowl of fresh water outside so that your puppy associates the garden with his natural needs.

Resist the urge to cover every inch of the floor with newspaper as puppy will defecate all over the place and become confused as to what is expected of him.

It is easier to train a puppy in the spring or summer when the back door can be left open, but no one said training a puppy would be easy. If you are worried about the cold weather then perhaps a dog and all that it entails to walk and train him is not for you?

It may take time to completely train your puppy but try to do it with praise rather than scolding. Do not believe old wives' tales, like rubbing his nose in any accident, as this will just frighten him.

House training is a work in progress! I'm using newspaper and puppy pads but am not overzealous at the moment (Matilda is 10 weeks old) as once she can go out after her second jab it will be sorted out very easily.

Kelly Rose Bradford

OTHER PETS

You may have another dog in the family. Sometimes an older
dog will teach the puppy where to go to the toilet and training
will be easy. Sometime the older dog copies the youngster and
you will have to train two dogs at once. Again, praise is the way
to train.

Older pets may become jealous of the new member of the family
so when puppy first comes home do not leave them alone.
Equally, try to share your time with both pets so that the older
one does not feel left out. This is very similar to bringing home a
new baby, apart from the fact that you cannot explain to the older
pet that they are still loved as much as when they were the 'only
child'.

Using a crate and spending time with both pets should quite
quickly reap dividends and you will soon have a happy household.
Sometimes it is the puppy that upsets the older pet and must be
trained not to bother the other animal all the time. Make sure
that the older pet has a bolt-hole to run to. Cats will climb up to
be above a puppy and observe the situation thoughtfully but an
older dog may not be able to escape the little dog and stress or
fear can make bad bedfellows. The older dog may have his own
crate or simply be able to sleep the other side of the dog gate. If
this is the case try to integrate the two dogs slowly using treats
and walks for the two animals to get to know each other. It is very
rare that two animals hate each other to the extent that one has to
leave home or the owner has to practise segregation for the next
ten years.

DISPOSAL OF DOG WASTE

How will you be disposing of the dog waste in your garden, flushing it down the toilet or perhaps down an outside drain? This is fine as long as you only have a small dog and you don't block the drains.

If you plan to put the dog waste out for the bin men to collect, check with your local council waste department first. My local council are prepared to dispose of dog waste as long as it is double-bagged and placed in with other household waste, but rules do vary.

I use biodegradable poo bags and place them in bins when out for a walk. At home I flush the poo from the garden down the toilet.

Anna Webb

DIY waste disposer

Purchase a large plastic dustbin with a secure lid, and carefully cut four large holes in the bottom of the bucket. Puncture smaller holes around the sides and half the way up the height of the bin.

Dig a hole in your garden which is one foot deeper than the bucket, and fill the hole with six inches of pea shingle. Top this up with larger pebbles and sit the dustbin on top so that when the lid is on it sites just above the level of the ground. Sit the bin into the hole and fill around the outside with more pea shingle to secure the bin in place. Use a bioactivator or septic tank starter as per the instructions as you gradually add your dog waste. Also flush with water occasionally to help solids disintegrate.

Note: This should be sited away from where children and pets play and not near to a vegetable plot or waterway.

Wormery

It is possible to recycle your dog waste in a ready-made wormery. The compost from the wormery should not be used on vegetables in the garden but is suitable for flower beds. The ready-made kits come with all ingredients and by following easy steps the worms will soon be processing your dog's waste and making suitable fertiliser for the garden.

A note of advice is not to put dog faeces into the wormery if your dog has recently been wormed, as it will kill all worms working in the wormery.

The author's thoughts

Homes that include a dog as part of the family should be safe and secure. Just as we would baby proof rooms we should puppy proof them. Breeders would do well to give a tip sheet to prospective puppy purchasers on this subject.

Cleaning up after our dogs is very important. We should also be aware of where the dog waste ends up – landfill sites and medical waste incinerators are some of the places used by council waste disposal services.

3

Early Days

In the early days of owning your puppy ground rules need to be made and followed religiously. It is not just the little dog that needs to know how to behave but you, your spouse, your children and any visitors to the home. Usually at the news there is a new puppy in the family visitors will swoop to touch, cuddle and completely bewilder the little dog. For the sake of future harmony in your home set some ground rules now and make sure everyone knows you mean business.

A CLEAN PUPPY

Nothing is nicer than a sweet smelling puppy that knows the difference between where to sleep and where to do his business. We looked at house training in the previous chapter so I will try not to repeat myself here. Some puppies take an age to get clean while others are very good from day one. The important point is not to get stressed and transmit this to the puppy. Praise him when he gets things right and do not worry when he makes a mistake. Use dog gates to keep him in an area that can be cleaned until you are sure he can be trusted not to leave a deposit in your bedroom or the living room.

It may upset your family's schedule for several weeks but if members of the family take turns to walk with the puppy into your garden after each meal or drink of water he will soon realise that gardens can be fun places and also somewhere to go to the toilet. Shutting him outside on his own can be frightening so be brave and go with him night and day and your efforts will soon be rewarded.

Pick up straight away as some dogs will walk their mess indoors or even try to eat it. Scented nappy sacks are cheap and easy to use for picking up after a dog, and they are also biodegradable. Keep a roll of kitchen paper by the back door to wipe any drips left on the puppy. Wet wipes are also a good idea and leave the little dog smelling sweet.

BASIC TRAINING

It is never too early to train your puppy in the basics of wearing a collar and being walked on a lead. Every puppy will grow whether it is a Yorkshire Terrier or a Great Dane so do not bother investing in an expensive collar and lead. Most pet shops supply puppy-sized sets that will see the puppy through the first weeks of living at home with you. A name tag with his name and your contact details should be on all collars just in case your puppy is lost or possibly escapes from your garden. By law all dogs should now be tagged when out in a public area so get into the habit of always having a tag on your dog's collar.

Remember that your puppy cannot be taken for walks or meet other dogs until he has been through the course of vaccinations. This can differ from vet to vet but the injections are usually administered two weeks apart with a space of two weeks before puppy can hit the street walking.

Some puppies are not keen on wearing a collar so place it on him just before feeding time or when you are playing so his attention is taken away from the novelty item hanging around his neck. Do not be tempted to fit it too loose as he may well pull it off and try to eat it or become caught when the collar hooks onto something and chokes him.

Some puppies are upset by a collar or lead. If yours is unhappy with the feel of a lead try using a ribbon as it is light and cannot be felt. Move gradually to a puppy-sized lead or a thin cord lead.

When in the garden and before playtime hook on the lead and coax puppy to walk by your left side. Do not drag or tug him along but use a friendly high voice to call his name. Never leave the other end of the lead hanging nor let him mouth the lead. Hold it taut and above his head and walk at a pace that would be at a brisk rate to his little legs. Remove the lead after a few minutes and praise him if he has behaved during his training. By the time puppy is over his vaccinations he will be lead trained and ready to walk happily outside his home.

EVERYDAY NOISES

By the time puppy comes home with you the breeder will have acclimatised him to everyday noises. Even so, your home and any outside noises will be strange to him. In the weeks that follow before puppy can be taken outside the home introduce him to noise such as the radio, television, washing machine and vacuum cleaner. Let him see that mops and brooms are not sticks to be played with or things that will hurt him. Sit in the garden with him so that outside noises become familiar.

Gradually introduce him to your front garden so he can see and hear cars. Cars are one of the most frightening things to a puppy. One of our dogs took ages to get used to buses as he had never seen one near his birth home. Each day our walks would follow a bus route and we would sit in the bus shelter until he accepted that these big red noisy things would not hurt him. It did take him a while to understand that people rode in these vehicles as he would hide whenever someone disembarked. After a month or so he enjoyed a ride on the bus to a park. In fact as an older dog it was very hard to make him walk past a bus stop as he wanted to join the queue.

CAR JOURNEYS

I will cover travelling with a dog in a later chapter (see pages 113–18) but even before puppy can go out for a walk there is no reason why he cannot sit in your car and get used to the movement of the vehicle. Introducing a dog to car journeys later in life can cause all kinds of behavioural problems ranging from continuous howling, frantic bids to escape or motion sickness, perhaps even all three. Sitting on the back seat with puppy while someone drives the car will show him that it is a safe and fun place to be. Remember also that quite often a puppy's first experience of car travel is when he is taken away from his mother and siblings so try to be gentle and sympathetic to his worries.

VISITORS

Your puppy is sure to attract a lot of attention when he first comes home. Everyone will want to meet the little bundle of fur. Try to encourage your visitors not to bring their own dogs to visit as your puppy is still vulnerable to infection at this stage if he has not had the full set of vaccinations. If visitors have dogs of their own encourage them to remove their shoes and to wash their hands before touching your dog. Better to be safe than have a sickly pup.

Puppies tire easily so stagger his fun time and also his visitors. Give him some peace and quiet in another room or in his cage if he is happy to snooze there. Some people assume it is funny to encourage puppy to bite and play tug of war with clothing as well as toys. Stop this immediately as tricks like that are easily learned and hard to stop. Point out to your visitors that puppy's little jaw and teeth are still soft and growing. Playing tugging games will simply ruin his mouth.

DISCIPLINE

Start as you mean to go on. Easily said when the dog weighs just a few pounds and is so cute. Mealtimes, playtime and bedtime should be adhered to from day one. You are the boss and you do not want an out of control dog that will not eat when food is given to him nor one who wants to play when it is bedtime.

There is no point in reprimanding a dog for something he did hours before. A dog should be told off (using a deep growling voice) within 15 seconds of any incident. NEVER slap a puppy or enforce discipline with violent actions.

Socialisation classes

These are quite a new initiative and are usually run by veterinary surgeries. The idea is for puppies of a similar age to meet at the vet's and get to know other dogs and other people. I'm in two minds about this as I feel it is far too early for puppies to be facing the possibility of catching something from outside the home. Better perhaps to train at home. A few weeks will not make a lot of difference to a dog that is likely to be with you for the next 15 years.

A GOOD VET

What makes a good vet? Someone who does not charge the earth for a consultation perhaps? Someone who has a surgery at the end of your road? With pet insurance so readily available vet fees should not be a problem and surely it is better to travel to a nice vet rather than go to a grumpy one in the next street. After all, if you have a life or death problem with your dog you rush to the nearest vet even if it isn't your usual one. Remember you can go to any vet. We do not have to register our pets and stay with one vet as we do with our doctor.

How to find a good vet

♦ Speak to fellow dog owners about their relationship with their vet and if they would recommend that surgery. What are the opening times? Are the staff friendly? Are they known to force branded dog food on their clients? The reception area of the surgery should not be a place to force-feed dog owners with political paperwork from charities or have shelves stocked with high-priced sacks of dog food.

♦ If you favour complementary treatment look for a vet that includes this in his practice.

♦ Use the internet to find local vets and read their websites. Are they informative and friendly? Do they tell you what you want to know? A snazzy all-singing all-dancing website does not mean that the vet is good – he may just spend his day on the internet!

♦ If the website intimidates you it may mean that the vet will. During our long campaign to retain the right to dock our dogs' tails I found that some vets were preaching to puppy owners and instilling their views in new dog owners. Remember you are buying their veterinary knowledge not their political views.

♦ Do not assume that if the veterinary surgery is part of a large chain that they are better than a small one-man band. I proved this wrong to the cost of my lovely dog Oliver's life. Ten years on I am still very bitter. These days I visit a vet who will sit on the floor and talk to my dog and is there 24/7 for us – small comfort for Oliver but great news for his children and grandchildren. Every person in the small surgery is there for the animals and is lovely to speak to; they never give the impression we are taking up too much of their time. They are there for us and our dogs. I'll add his name to the list at the end of this book just in case you are fortunate to live in North Kent.

♦ Internet search engines are an excellent way to find out about good vets and bad vets. Also use the search facility on local newspaper websites as a news story, good or bad, can alter your impression on your choice of vet. Spend time searching out news on the vets in your area. It could be an eye-opener.

♦ Finally be prepared to move to another vet if you are unhappy. You need not tell them, just book in to another.

TRAINING CLASSES

All dogs need training, or perhaps I should say all dog owners need training. Don't assume that because you are not intending to compete in obedience or working trials, or do not want to enter the show ring, that you need not go to training classes. The beginner's class in both obedience and show ring training teaches the dog and the owner the basics of being in tune with each other and how to work together as a team. Training the dog to walk and run to heel, sit, stay and not drag on the lead or run away are all tricks we need to know if we want to socialise with our dogs and enjoy each other's company.

Speak to the secretary of the training club to find out what they can do for your new puppy. Ask at what age they will take on a puppy and if they will let the whole family come along to be trained as well. It's not good just having one person in the family who can control the dog.

How to find a dog training class

♦ Ask at your veterinary surgery if they know of local training clubs.

♦ Pet stores will have a display of all kinds of local pet clubs.

♦ Dog owners in your locality will know of the best clubs. If you spot a well-behaved dog ask the owner where they attend training.

♦ Join a breed club for your breed. Meeting fellow breed owners at a club can help you train your type of dog alongside those who know the breed well. If you want to exhibit your dog it can help immensely to train with fellow breed owners.

♦ The Kennel Club holds a list of registered training clubs for many types of dog sport. Details of the Kennel Club can be found at the end of this book.

We have travelled many miles to good training classes where there are trainers sympathetic to our dogs' obstinate ways. On another occasion we joined a club where there were other Old English Sheepdogs and owners and we worked together to train our dogs for the show ring.

We attended training classes with Hank but not with Eric. I think they're essential. Hank learned to interact with other dogs and we learned things we hadn't even thought of ourselves. It's easy to be a bit arrogant and think you're above puppy classes but they are as much for owners as dogs.

Hazel Davis

LATCH KEY PUPPIES

There is no reason to leave your dog either shut in the garden all day long or left alone in the home. In fact only bad dog owners would do such a thing and if a breeder was aware your dog was to be left for long periods each day you would most likely be on their blacklist of undesirable owners.

Sometimes circumstances change after you bring your puppy home. You may find that you are not able to be at home and he is left for long lengths of time. This is not good for any age of dog. Training cannot be undertaken and a dog cannot be exercised. Feeding is left to first thing in the morning and last thing at night. The puppy will start to chew; he will become distressed and cry. Crate training cannot be followed and he should not be shut in a cage for long hours at a time. Neighbours too can be inconvenienced with a crying and barking dog next door.

This may have meant in years gone by that you would be handing back your puppy to the breeder or leaving him at an animal rescue centre. These days there is an answer: doggy day care. More and more of these centres are opening up across the country. Sometimes it is a boarding kennel offering the service or perhaps someone setting up a dedicated service. You can drop puppy off and collect him after work. His feeding regime will be followed and his training continued, which will suit many people who need to work and also want a dog.

Alternatively there are puppy-walking and dog-sitting services that can come to your home and work with puppy while you are away from home. All can offer references.

To find these services look in pet magazines for national pet care services or search online for suitable services to fit your needs.

A doggy day care centre should not just be a place where puppy is run off his legs playing with other dogs, nor should he be route marched through fields and lanes all day. There should be times when he is trained on a one-to-one basis and times when he can sleep or rest alone. His diet should be observed as per your instructions and you should be informed if anything untoward happens to him during the time he is left. In fact your puppy's day should be very much like a child's day when they are left in a day nursery, apart from finger painting!

WALKIES AND EXERCISING

A puppy's bones are very soft. His joints will not tolerate miles of brisk walking every day. Once his imposed vaccination period is over treat the daily walks with care. The outside world will be very scary to a little dog – vehicle noises, other people and other dogs will either be interesting or downright petrifying depending on how brave your puppy is.

By the time he is ready to venture out into the big wide world he should be able to wear his collar and lead and not be bothered by them. Your practice walks up and down the garden will have paid off and he will not pull away from the lead or scratch at his collar.

With a pocket of small treats step out onto the path and walk at a slow pace using encouraging words if he seems startled. A small treat of baked liver held in front of his nose will tempt him on but do not stuff food into him at every step. Try not to pick him up and carry him on his walk as he may begin to expect this every day.

When approaching a road encourage him to sit and wait. Wait longer than necessary so he gets to see the cars and lorries whizzing by. Walk him over the road and then praise him and give him a small treat. Gradually the verbal praise will be enough so food is not expected every few minutes.

It is quite natural for a small puppy to want to jump up to greet anyone that talks to him. After all the happy voice is quite a few feet higher than him and he wants to be able to get close to the new friend. Your puppy should not stand on his back legs either jumping up at humans or at the fence for two reasons. The first is that puppy may one day turn into a very large dog that will be able to knock over children and frighten people who are not so keen on our four-legged friends. The second reason is that his bones and joints are still forming and any undue pressure on hip joints can lead to health problems in his adult years. Walking too far will also cause the same problem. Short and often is the answer. If you are unsure of how long each walk should be speak to the breeder of your puppy and also check with the breed club. These people want to help you and your puppy lead a long and happy life together so use their knowledge.

The author's thoughts

If owners work hard in the first weeks a puppy joins his new family there is less chance of unsociable behaviour when the dog has grown to his full size.

4

The health of your puppy

Caring for a new puppy can be time consuming. Not only do we have to feed and exercise the new member of our family but we must be responsible for his health and wellbeing.

GENERAL OBSERVATIONS

Lumps bumps and sore spots can be found with daily handling of your puppy through play, bathing and grooming. Check your dog's mouth and teeth – the gums should be pink and healthy; white gums are a sign that the dog is in poor health or shock if he has been injured or collapsed. There are products on the market to clean a dog's teeth although a nice juicy marrowbone is far better and a more enjoyable way to keep teeth free of plaque.

Check the ears for excessive wax. This can be cleaned gently with a cotton bud or ear wipes purchased from a pet store. Never poke into the ear cavity as this can cause distress to the dog as well as permanent hearing problems.

A puppy should get used to having his paws checked as there will be times throughout his life when nails need to be trimmed or hair clipped from between the pads. Regularly check that foreign bodies are not caught between the pads. Chewing gum, tar and small stones can cause problems walking. Grass seeds can easily work under the nails and into the skin. These can travel into the body causing infection and irritation – left unchecked they can require a major operation when they are removed.

The puppy will wriggle when first being checked over but regular handling will gradually lead to acceptance of these procedures.

SPECIFIC BREED PROBLEMS

Some purebred dogs do have health problems, although this is not necessarily in every dog of that breed. Inherited problems have been highlighted within some breeds of dogs. Breeders, along with the breed clubs, the Kennel Club Health and Breeders Services Department and canine health authorities, are striving to rid the breeds concerned of these problems. Sometimes it is possible to breed with a dog that is a carrier of an inherited health problem as long as the full health history is known of both the dam and sire. This book is a basic guide to buying a puppy and will point you in the right direction to find out about health screening and control of diseases and problems in a chosen breed. News on health procedures is changing all the time and if you are ever in doubt about the health of your chosen breed then speak to the Kennel Club or breed club for the latest news.

Accredited breeders

The Kennel Club holds a register of accredited breeders. The breeders on this register have to undertake all health screening procedures recommended for their breed. Documents regarding the health screening will be available for you to see when visiting the breeders. However, if a breeder has not joined the Accredited Breeder scheme it does not make them a bad breeder. Most good breeders follow guidelines that will make and keep their breed happy and healthy.

Breed health initiatives

DNA screening is now undertaken for many of the UK's pedigree breeds of dog. The list is far too long to include in this book and would probably be out of date within months. Contact the Kennel Club for a list or visit their website to read up on your chosen breed.

BVA/KC Health Schemes

Along with the Kennel Club the British Veterinary Association runs screening schemes to detect signs of inherited diseases such as elbow dysplasia, hip dysplasia and eye diseases in breeds that are susceptible to these health problems. The results of the screening are placed on record at the Kennel Club and show on puppy and litter registration documents.

Note: It is possible to check out all health screening that has been registered at the Kennel Club on the parents of your dog. The Kennel Club now has a programme on their website called 'Dog Health Test Search' where you add the name of the dog (or stud book number) and the information is revealed. The breeder of the puppies will give you the names of the dam and sire of the litter when you telephone to make your first enquiry.

NEUTERING

There is so much spoken about neutering puppies within months of their birth. Obviously this is done so that there are no unwanted puppies once the dog is old enough to breed. Bitches can breed from their first season which in some breeds is as early as six months. This is far too young for any dog to care for a litter apart from being mature enough to cope with such a monumental change to their lives. With a bitch coming into season at the most twice each year is it too much to ask of an owner to keep the dog indoors and away from male dogs for ten days each time?

Male dogs will become interested in bitches before they are one year old. Any good dog owner would never let their dog wander and be in the position to mate with a bitch, so ask yourself why put a dog through surgery at a young age if it is not likely to meet a dog of the opposite sex for the few weeks each year when they are able to mate? If you are neutering your dog because he is showing aggressive tendencies or you feel he is dominant there is no reason to think that neutering will cure this.

Some vets encourage new owners to have their puppies neutered before the first season. I prefer to wait until the bitch has had at least two seasons before considering this as an option for birth control. We are told that neutering lessens the chances of mammary cancer in later life but I want my girls to grow and mature before facing a major operation. After all, as vigilant and caring owners, if our dogs have any lumps or bumps we will take them to the vet to have them investigated and not assume that the neutering procedure has given them a magic 'get out of jail card' to protect their health later in life.

VACCINATION

Puppies cannot go out into the outside world until they have had their full course of vaccinations. These are given as two injections usually two weeks apart. The vaccinations start when the puppy is as young as eight weeks but this can differ slightly according to the size of the dog or the decision of the veterinary practice. Once the second injection is given the puppy should remain at home for a further two weeks before he can start meeting other dogs and people and beginning his fun-filled life.

Vaccination covers your puppy for four major infectious diseases: hepatitis, canine distemper, parvovirus and leptospirosis. It is also possible, and highly advisable, to include kennel cough, which can kill young puppies and older dogs. If you plan at any time to place your dog into boarding kennels it is a requirement that the dog has his kennel cough shots up to date, with proof of the vaccination from your vet.

Vaccinations should be kept up to date with yearly boosters from your vet. Keep your dog's vaccination records safe in case you move to another vet or need reminding of when they become due. At the time the booster vaccination is given your vet will also check your dog over for any other health problems and discuss worming and preventative treatment for other parasites.

The alternative route

Just as many of us follow an alternative lifestyle and avoid chemicals and drugs, so do many dog owners. Some owners have just the initial puppy vaccinations and then have homeopathic treatments in the following years. Other breeders start the young puppies on homeopathic treatment from just a few weeks of age and leave the choice up to the new owners whether they wish to follow the traditional route or the homeopathic one.

I've tried both methods mainly because I lost a dog at the age of five when he died from an auto-immune disease after a booster injection. My choice these days is to have those first puppy vaccinations and after that I use homeopathic treatment. I have two very healthy twelve-year-old dogs in my home at present that have never had a chemical injected into their bodies. I have a very good vet who practises homeopathy and I have faith in his treatment of my dogs.

PARASITES

It is not uncommon for dogs to catch internal or external parasites. By keeping an eye on your puppy you can ensure that parasites do not take hold and can be dealt with swiftly and effectively. There are products that can be purchased from the vet that are absorbed into the skin so that fleas and ticks are never a problem. As previously mentioned, I am not in favour of drenching my dogs in chemicals just in case something hops onto them and even with a household of large hairy dogs we have never had a parasite problem that required chemical warfare.

Symptoms

Parasites will show in a puppy in various ways. A pot belly and a ravenous appetite can be signs of a worm infestation along with possible sightings of worms in the faeces. An itchy coat and black flecks, which are dried blood, are often the first signs with fleas. The coat will be dull and puppy will be generally listless if these are left untreated. Amazingly within days of treatment he will look bright-eyed and bushy-tailed once more.

Here are a few of the more common parasites along with tips on how to get rid of them.

External parasites

Cheyletiella mite

These mites look like white moving dandruff on the dog. Skin can be red and there is a slight itchiness with small crusty spots. Eggs are left on the hair shaft. The lifecycle can be between 20 and 35 days on the host dog and the adult mite can live off the host dog for up to two weeks.

Diagnosis: This is done from skin scrapings or collecting the mites on sticky tape for analysis.

Treatment: The dog should be treated by the vet and can usually be cured with a treatment of specialist shampoo over four to six weeks. If this does not cure the problem there are further treatments available. Cats, rabbits and humans can also catch this mite.

Dermodex mange mite

These mites are passed to puppies from the mother only in the first weeks of life although some strains can be caught by a puppy up to the age of one year. Localised mange will appear as bald patches on the face of the dog whereas the generalised variety can cover the whole of the body.

Diagnosis: Bald patches, scaly skin and infection.

Treatment: The bitch should not be bred from again and should preferably be spayed once she has been treated for the condition. A prescribed medication from the vet will be needed to cure this condition although in some dogs it may be more persistent.

Fleas

Fleas are probably the most common parasite found on a dog, but are easily treated. If you check during grooming the best places to spot the flea are at the back of the head (near the occiput), on the shoulders or at the base of the tail. You will find that your dog seems to have a place on his body favoured by the flea that will differ to another dog.

Diagnosis: Flea dirt left on the skin and possible sightings of the flea scurrying or jumping on the coat.

Treatment: It is possible to buy a product from your vet that will keep your dog free of fleas at all times simply by breaking a phial of liquid in the area of his shoulder blades. I prefer the older method of careful grooming and dabbing any fleas found with a 50/50 mix of water and washing up liquid. This seems to paralyse any movement in the flea giving you time to pick it off the coat and drop it into a bowl of washing up liquid. I keep a small dish of the washing up liquid close to hand when flea hunting and use it to dab the flea and then drown it. A bath with a good flea shampoo afterwards usually cures the problem.

Fleas can live away from the dog so if there is a serious infestation all furnishings should be treated. Sprays and powders for this purpose can be purchased from supermarkets, pet stores and chemists.

One species of tapeworm can use the flea as a host. If the adult flea is ingested by a dog or human it can grow into a tapeworm inside the stomach. Segments can come out and be seen to wriggle. An off-the-shelf remedy easily cures the problem for both dog and owner.

Harvest mites

Picked up in long grass or near to bushes and undergrowth in warmer weather, these mites are usually found on the feet or ears of dogs.

Diagnosis: Seen as orange/red clusters of dust-like areas that can grow in size before dropping off. They can cause intense itching in some dogs.

Treatment: There is not an off-the-shelf treatment for harvest mites although a product called Thornits has been found to be highly efficient in clearing the problem.

Lice

Dog lice are not that common in this country. The lice look like small dots of dirt on the skin of the dog. The lice cannot be caught by the human owner. It can cause severe itching and anaemia in the animal.

Diagnosis: The small spots of 'dirt' do not come away easily when washing the dog.

Treatment: Consult your vet but this infestation can usually be treated with pyrethrin-based shampoo used over several weeks.

Sarcoptic mange (fox mite)

This mite is carried by foxes. The mites can be picked up by dogs without making contact with the fox as the mite can live away from the host.

Diagnosis: By a vet as it is very similar to other mange with bald itchy patches.

Treatment: It can take a while to rid the dog completely of this mange. A good diet and supplement can help a dog recover quickly.

Ticks

Ticks feed on the blood of the host and drop off when they are full of blood. Dogs that root around in undergrowth tend to pick up ticks on the nose and face. The tick needs to be pulled away from the dog but care must be taken that the head is not left buried in the skin as infection will remain. There are gadgets that can be bought that look like tweezers that hold the lice so they come away with one pull. I use tweezers for the odd time this happens and then dab the area with surgical spirit afterwards. A dab of Vaseline used to cover the tick can have a suffocating effect and cause the tick to drop off. Make sure that the tick is killed or it will continue to attach itself to your pets.

I was once told by an old dog man to simply dab the tick with the end of a cigarette and it would drop off. This could be dangerous to the dog and also the owner if they have to take up smoking just to be rid of a tick.

Internal parasites

Lungworm

The lungworm (sometimes called French heartworm) can live in the heart and major blood vessels of the dog and can have serious or even fatal consequences. The lungworm parasite is carried by snails and slugs so if your dog likes to eat these in your garden it is time to stop this habit. Usually news of lungworm being found in the area spreads quickly and owners should be vigilant. Foxes can carry this parasite and play their part in spreading this nasty disease. Dogs once infected also spread the disease through their faeces.

Diagnosis: If you are concerned that lungworm is in your area your vet can run tests to check your dog before symptoms show. Usually poor blood clotting, anaemia, lethargy and breathing problems lead the owner and vet to think a dog is infested with this parasite.

Treatment: Lungworm is not cured by the usual worming medication. Your vets can prescribe a drug that is dropped onto the skin between the shoulder blades that will cure a dog that is not in the later stages of infection. Keep your garden free of faeces and have all your dogs checked by your vet if one dog becomes infected.

Roundworm

Toxocara canis and toxocara leonine are the most common forms of worm infestation found in dogs and puppies. Toxocara canis is the worm usually found in the puppy, and is passed from the mother either via the uterus or through her milk. A bitch should be wormed before mating and puppies put onto a mild programme of worming paste as they are weaned at three to four weeks.

Diagnosis: Quite often the worms can be seen in the puppy's faeces. The puppy will not be thriving as well as it should be and may have a pot belly.

Treatment: Follow the worming procedure for the weight of your dog as shown on the packet of pills and dose according to the weight and age of the puppy. A satisfying show of dead worms will be expelled from the puppy. Dogs should be wormed every three to six months or when infestation is present.

Be aware that humans can be affected by these roundworm larvae when accidentally ingested. There is a very slight chance that the larvae will travel around the body and lodge in the eye causing eye problems and sometimes blindness. This is passed by cats as well as dogs.

Note: Toxocara leonine is not passed from the mother to the puppies but instead the eggs are ingested.

Tapeworms
See above under 'fleas'.

FIRST AID FOR DOGS

When a dog is taken ill or has an accident it is imperative that you get him to a vet as soon as possible, or have a vet call on you. Until a vet is found there are some things that you can do.

If an accident should happen or the dog collapses away from home call the police as they will have the contact details of an emergency vet or a nearby animal hospital or surgery. They will also be able to help you with the injured dog.

Remember that a usually docile animal may be scared and in pain and will act out of character. The chances are that they will lash out at you so use a lead, a tie or a belt to muzzle the dog but make sure that air passages are clear and the dog is not put under more stress by being muzzled.

If the dog has been hit by a car ask someone to control the traffic until you can make the injured dog comfortable or arrange to move him somewhere safer. Ask onlookers to step back in order to keep the dog calm while you wait for help.

You may be able to undertake some first aid while waiting for a vet.

Cuts

Never add any substance to a cut but cover with a clean pad and administer pressure to the area to stop the flow of blood. For grazes and small cuts clean the area with a saline solution and cover to stop the animal licking the wound.

Burns

Never burst blisters or administer creams to a burn. Rinse with cool water for at least five minutes or until veterinary help arrives.

Drowning

Do not dive into a lake or river after a dog without considering your own safety. We often hear of owners drowning while trying to save a much-loved pet and the dog then clambering ashore.

If the animal is not showing signs of life hold them by the back legs and swing from side to side. This will force water from the lungs and the dog may start breathing. If the dog is not breathing stretch him on his side and check for anything that may be blocking the airway.

If there is not a heartbeat try to administer pressure to the heart in regular bursts. Try to be careful with smaller dogs as this could break a rib. Next close the dog's mouth, pull the neck out to extend it and blow up the nose until the dog gasps for air. This can be repeated.

While carrying out any procedures make sure that someone is calling for help from a vet or the police.

Moving an injured dog

If you need to transport an injured dog to the veterinary surgery use a car blanket or an overcoat to carry the dog. Use the blanket as you would a stretcher for a larger dog aiming not to hurt the injured area when you move the animal. Try to have someone help you carry the injured dog and sit with him in the car while you drive.

Mobile phone

Programme your vet's telephone number into your mobile phone. If travelling with your dog ensure that you have the number of a vet from the area you are visiting to hand just in case of emergency.

First aid kit

A canine first aid kit should be kept at home and also in the car when your dog travels with you. A first aid kit can be purchased from pet stores and veterinary surgeries but can be made as follows:

- A waterproof box with well-fitting lid

- Packet of bandages

- A self-clinging bandage

- Adhesive tape

- Cover or compress for wounds

- Alcohol swabs

- A syringe for cleaning or feeding

- Soft muzzle

- ◆ Spare lead with collar

- ◆ Tweezers

- ◆ Small pair of scissors

- ◆ Flea or lice comb

- ◆ Latex gloves

- ◆ Small bottle of antiseptic cleanser or wipes

The author's thoughts

Your vet should be someone who you can talk to, not someone that you are afraid of. He or she should be there to guide you with any health-related problems you may have. They should NEVER inflict their own political or breed-related opinions on you. They should respect your choice of health care and the views of your dog's breeder. Remember that a vet is not for life and you are free to shop around for a new vet if you are unhappy with the service they provide. You are also at liberty to report your vet to his governing body if you feel your pet's best interests have not been considered correctly.

5

Food for Life

When you first meet the breeder of your puppy or attend a
meeting at the rescue centre, the puppy's diet will be explained
to you, hopefully in some detail. It is usual for the breeder to give
you a sample of the food if they are following a manufactured
brand. The manufacturers provide the food along with
information leaflets in order to continue selling to the owners of
the puppies just as they did to the breeder.

You should have several weeks before you collect your puppy,
giving you time to source a local stockist of the food. Mail order
can also be an option but do not buy large sacks of the food as
you will encounter stage problems and also the food may go stale
if you have a small breed of dog and a 20 kilo sack of food.

Your breeder will show you how to feed the puppy and supply
you with a sheet of paper that shows how much and when to give

the food; this is called the diet sheet and should be followed religiously when puppy first goes home with you. Do not be tempted to feed another product to your puppy especially if you have other dogs that eat a different brand or style of feed.

CHANGE OF DIET

When changing any dog to a new brand of food or to another feeding regime take at least two weeks to change gradually to the new food. This will get the dog used to the new food without fear of an upset stomach or diarrhoea. Some dogs can be very fussy with food, but you should persevere as they will eat when they are hungry. Do not start making fancy or expensive meals just to please your dog, or your conscience.

IS MY DOG THE RIGHT WEIGHT?

With a growing puppy there will be times when puppy may feel thin but hopefully never fat. A thin dog, if healthy, will simply need the quantity of food in each meal increased slightly. A good guide to whether your dog is too thin or fat is to feel his backbone and ribs. If they are too prominent he is too thin. If the ribs are covered too well and he feels heavy on the shoulders he is too fat. Cut back on his food or try replacing some of the biscuit with finely-shredded carrots and white cabbage.

HOW MANY MEALS?

This is where you must read the breeder's guidelines as they know what the puppy has been consuming each day. In the first weeks of life straight after weaning your puppy would have been on six meals each day. By the time he comes home with you this will be four meals each day. By the time he is six months old he will be eating more at each meal but will have reduced to the two meals each day that he will have for the rest of his life. There may be times in pregnancy or illness when you revert back to feeding your dog more meals but in a smaller volume.

WHAT SHOULD MY PUPPY BE EATING?

Even when your breeder is feeding a complete food there may be a variation on how it is served. This is what you should follow. The puppies I've bred do not eat a complete diet when they are weaned. They lap on baby porridge and puréed savoury meat and vegetables, gradually moving on to eating proper food at every meal. The type of diet they eat over six meals each day is:

◆ Weetabix with warmed milk

◆ Puppy porridge

◆ Scrambled egg

◆ Mashed pilchards in oil

◆ Small balls of raw minced beef

◆ Minced chicken, turkey or lamb or beef simmered in stock and served with some puppy mixer biscuit

◆ Fresh water

◆ I will also introduce bones and dog biscuits to their diet.

My puppies have always drunk fresh cow's milk from an early age and I've never had a problem with their digestion. I feel this is because they are introduced to lots of foods at an early age rather than a manufactured diet.

If you feel that you would like to feed your puppy on the above food, introduce it gradually rather than change the food in one day.

TYPES OF FOOD

There are many types of dog food and many kinds of feeding regimes. None are wrong; you must consider what suits your dog, your lifestyle, your beliefs and your purse.

Complete food

This food is what I class as convenient food. Open the sack and serve to your dog. There are some quality brands on the market that are free from additives of any kind so you can be assured that your dog is not consuming chemicals such as colorants and preservatives that cannot be good for him when eaten on a daily basis.

If this is your favoured choice of feeding read up on the brand of your choice. Most have a website that not only gives you all sorts of information on the growth of a dog and feeding guidelines but also allows you, the dog owner, to ask questions. The good manufacturers of dog food can be found with large stands at all major dog shows. I know you may not wish to exhibit your dog but go and visit Crufts, Discover Dogs or one of the many championship dog shows that are held around the country. Speak to the sales advisors and ask for a sample of the food so that you can try before you buy.

It is not as simple as buying a sack of complete food. The choice is quite worrying as there are diets for all ages of the dog as well as different sizes of dog and even breeds with some brands. You almost need a GCSE in feeding complete food to your dog!

Canned meat and mixer biscuit

Just like complete food there is good food and bad food hidden inside these cans with happy dogs on the labels. Read the labels carefully but do not believe all you read. Some food manufacturers reckon you need three cans each day for some dogs – this is far too much and can lead to your owning an obese dog. Use your own judgement when feeding your dog.

Some canned dog food looks quite unappealing and consists of preformed squares of 'meat' in very runny gravy. Try to buy a canned meat that has meat rather than gravy and cereal. If I do use a canned food for my dogs I prefer Butcher's Tripe. I've never had a problem with it and served it with a plain mixer biscuit (plain meaning one with hardly any additives). I do like to make my own mixer biscuit but when I don't have time I fall back on Laughing Dog terrier bite mixer. This size of mixer is fine for larger breeds.

BARF diet

BARF is an acronym for Biologically Appropriate Raw Food and was developed by vet, Dr Ian Billinghurst. The aim of the diet is to feed raw natural products to your dog. Meat, offal, vegetables, bones, fruit, egg and other ingredients make up this energy-packed style of feeding your dog. This is a very popular way to feed a dog and does show results. You can find out more on their website, at www.barfworld.com

Raw Meaty Bones (RMB) diet

This is another raw diet and one that is gaining popularity. The diet is what it says, feeding your dog a raw diet comprising of meat, fish and game on the bone. What could be healthier? For more information, visit www.rawmeatybones.com

MAKE YOUR OWN DOG FOOD

I like to make my dogs' food from scratch, in fact I wrote about it in *Canine Cuisine* (How To Books). Raw and cooked main meals, my own mixer biscuit, training treats, everyday dog biscuits and celebration food, I cover it all. It beats giving your dog table scraps and cooking for the dog can be done when you are cooking for the family.

I find that children enjoy making biscuits for their dog and it instils an awareness of dog care at an early age if a child takes part in the feeding routine.

Here are a few recipes to get you cooking for your dog:

Molly's Milk Bone Biccies

Our youngest dog Molly has a tendency to put on weight. There's no denying the fact that she is a couch potato in the form of an Old English Sheepdog. I bake these tasty biscuits and use the smallest bone-shaped cutters I have so that she has her treat diet-sized.

Ingredients
½ mug beef suet
1 mug hot water

½ mug dried milk powder
4 mugs malted wheat grain flour
2 eggs
1 egg white

To make

Preheat oven to 180°C, Gas Mark 4

In a large mixing bowl add the beef suet and pour the hot water on top. Stir until suet has melted. Allow to cool slightly before adding the rest of the ingredients as follows.

Add the milk powder, stirring all the time followed by half of the flour.

Beat the two eggs and add to the mixture.

Add the rest of the flour to form a firm dough. You may need to add a little water if the mix is too stiff.

Turn out onto a floured surface and roll to half an inch in depth.

Using your bone-shaped cutter, cut the milk biscuit shapes and place on a lightly greased baking tray.

Place onto the centre shelf of your oven and bake for 50 minutes or until hard.

Remove from the oven and transfer to a cooling tray. Immediately brush each biscuit with egg white to give a shiny gloss to the biscuit.

When cool store in an airtight container.

Note: The smaller the biscuit the less baking time required.

Buster's Bacon Bites

Our Buster is a big cuddly dog who loves nothing more than sharing our food. He is particularly interested when bacon is being fried so this recipe was designed to suit him. He did appreciate the gesture!

Ingredients
1 250g pack of bacon pieces
5 eggs
4 mugs organic wholemeal flour
1 mug of milk

To make
Preheat oven to 200°C, Gas Mark 6

Chop the bacon into small pieces and fry in a large non-stick frying pan until they are crispy. When cool tip the bacon and residue of fat into a large mixing bowl.

Add the flour and stir.

Beat the eggs and add to the bacon and flour mix.

Gradually add the milk and stir well to break down any lumps in the flour. You should have a dropping consistency.

Drop heaped spoonfuls onto a greased baking tray and place in the oven to cook. The portion size can be varied to match the size of your dog. The biscuits are ready when they are firm to the touch.

If you turn off the oven when cooking has finished these Bacon Bites will harden overnight.

Alternatively you could cook these on top of the cooker on a griddle but they are best served hard and crispy.

Note: This is an ideal recipe for the cheaply-priced bacon scraps seen in most supermarkets.

Hayley's Hearts

Lamb hearts are a good source of nutrition and dogs love them. Our Hayley loved this meal and it was a favourite extra meal when she was expecting her litter of puppies. The recipe must have been good as she had nine healthy sheepdog babies, many of which reached over 14 years of age.

Ingredients
1 lamb's heart
1 tablespoon vegetable oil
1 lamb stock cube
1 potato
1 large carrot
2 mugs of water
1 tablespoon of gravy granules

To make
Cut the lamb's heart into one-inch cubes.

Heat the vegetable oil in a heavy-based pan and add the cubed lamb. Cook gently until browned on all sides.

Peel and dice the potato and carrot and add to the pan along with the stock cube and water.

Bring to the boil and leave to simmer for one hour or until the meat is tender.

Add the gravy granules to thicken and remove from heat to cool.

Serve with home-made mixer biscuit. Delicious!

This recipe can be frozen in small portions ready to reheat when desired.

Lovely Lamb

Cheaper cuts of meat that are slow cooked are tender enough even for the older dogs.

Ingredients
2 breasts of lamb
1 tablespoon vegetable oil
½ small onion
2 lamb stock cubes
3 mugs of water
1 clove of garlic
6 carrots
1 mug of frozen peas
1 teaspoon dried rosemary
3 tablespoons of cornflour

To make
Preheat the oven to 180°C, Gas Mark 4
(or use a slow cooker)

Cut the lamb into even-sized chunks between the bones.

Heat the oil and add the lamb, sealing all sides of the meat.

Finely chop the onion and the garlic and add to the pan. Stir until the onion is soft but not brown.

Wash and slice the carrot into thick chunks. Add to the pan with the meat. Add the stock cubes, rosemary and water and bring to a simmer.

Transfer to an ovenproof dish or the slow cooker and leave to cook slowly in the oven for three hours, or longer.

Remove from the oven and pull the bones from the meat. They should just fall away and discarded.

Mix the cornflour with a little water and stir until you have a lump-free paste. Stir into the casserole until it thickens.

Add the frozen peas.

Allow to cool and then divide into dog-sized portions.

Store in freezer bags and label.

Christmas Turkey Dinner

An ideal meal to have ready in the freezer so your dog can enjoy his Christmas meal with you. Add vegetables from the table and ready-made mixer biscuit.

Ingredients
1 tablespoon of vegetable oil
500g turkey mince
2 mugs of water

1 chicken or turkey stock cube
½ mug of sage and onion stuffing mix
2 tablespoons of turkey flavoured gravy granules
12 pork cocktail sausages
4 slices of streaky bacon

To make
Preheat oven to 200°C, Gas Mark 6

Heat the oil in a deep saucepan.

Add the turkey mince and cook for ten minutes until slightly brown.

Crumble in the stock cubes and add the water.

Bring to the boil and allow to simmer for 30 minutes on a low heat.

Remove from the heat and add the sage and onion mix. Add extra hot water if necessary as the mix should be thick but fluid. Add the gravy granules.

Transfer to an ovenproof dish and place in the oven for 45 minutes.

Meanwhile cut each rasher of streaky bacon into three and wrap a piece around each cocktail sausage. Place under the grill on a low heat and cook until the bacon is brown. Remove and leave to cool.

Remove the casserole from the oven and allow to cool.

Place portions of the turkey meal into containers and divide the sausages among the meals.

Freeze until needed.

Roast Vegetables and Chicken

This meal uses many ingredients that you would have in your freezer and vegetable store.

Ingredients

3 tablespoons of olive oil
6 chicken thighs with the bone removed
2 large potatoes
1 red onion
2 large carrots
1 parsnip
10 baby sweetcorn
1 tablespoon of dried rosemary
1 tablespoon garlic granules
1 mug hot water
1 tablespoon chicken gravy granules or cornflour

To make

Preheat the oven to 220°C, Gas Mark 7

In a frying pan heat a little of the oil and brown the chicken. Transfer to a deep baking tray.

Wash the vegetables and chop into large pieces. Scatter them among the chicken pieces.

Sprinkle the rosemary and garlic granules over the prepared dish followed by the rest of the olive oil.

Place in the hot oven for 45 minutes taking care to turn the vegetables and chicken so they do not burn.

Remove from the heat and allow to cool.

Divide the food into dog-sized portions.

Return the tray to the top of the cooker and add a mug of hot water to deglaze the tray. Add gravy granules or cornflour to make a gravy. When cool carefully tip a little into each container and then freeze.

Note: Foil containers with lids are ideal for this recipe.

Peanut Butter Pup Cakes

Ingredients

3 mugs of wholemeal flour
1 tablespoon baking powder
2 vegetable stock cubes
1 egg
½ mug vegetable oil
1 small jar of crunchy peanut butter
1 small jar of smooth peanut butter
Water to mix

To make

Preheat the oven to 200°C, Gas Mark 6

Lightly grease a muffin tin with vegetable oil.

Sift the flour and baking powder.

Crumble in the two vegetable stock cubes.

Beat the egg well and add to the mix.

Stir in the vegetable oil and the small jar of crunchy peanut butter.

The mix should resemble a cake mix. If it is too runny add more flour. If it is too stiff add more water.

Divide the mix into the muffin tin taking care to only three-quarter fill each section.

Place in the middle of the oven and bake for 20 minutes or until a skewer comes out clean when slid into a muffin.

Turn out onto a cooling tray.

When completely cool swirl the top of each with the smooth peanut butter and serve to your pup.

Ahhh! Lamb Birthday Cake

A tasty meaty treat for your dog's birthday dinner.

Ingredients
500g lamb mince
4 eggs
1 mug self-raising flour
½ mug of porridge oats
¼ mug vegetable oil
2 carrots
A handful of fresh parsley

Topping
1 tub of low fat cream cheese
1 packet of doggy chocs

To make

Preheat the oven to 200°C, Gas Mark 6

Place the lamb mince into a large mixing bowl. Beat the eggs and stir into the lamb until well combined.

Grate the carrots and finely chop the parsley.

Add the flour, oats, vegetable oil, carrots and parsley to the lamb mixture. And stir until all ingredients have been combined.

Tip the mix into a deep cake tin – a silicon one is ideal for a dog cake as the cake comes out easily and the container does not need to be greased before use.

Place into the centre of the preheated oven and cook for 45 minutes or until a skewer comes out clean when placed into the centre of the cake.

When cooked put the cake onto a cooling rack and when cold turn upside down to remove the cake from the container.

To decorate

Spread the low fat cream cheese over the top of the cake and using a fork make peaks like snow drifts across the cake. Add doggy choc drops to the top of each peak before serving to your birthday dog.

I mentioned making my own mixer biscuit earlier in this chapter. This is a favourite recipe.

Garlic Flavoured Mixer Biscuit

The garlic in this mixer biscuit recipe will give more flavour to the accompanying meat meal.

Ingredients

6 mugs of wholemeal flour
2 mugs of porridge oats
3 beef stock cubes
1 mug of hot water
4 eggs
3 tablespoons of garlic granules
Cold water

To make

Preheat oven to 200°C, Gas Mark 6

Tip the wholemeal flour and porridge oats into a large mixing bowl.

Crumble the stock cubes into the hot water and stir until dissolved. Leave to cool.

Beat the eggs and add to the flour and oats along with the stock cube mix.

Continue mixing until you have a firm dough, adding cold water if needed.

Turn out onto a floured surface and roll out to ¼ inch thickness.

Placed the rolled out pastry onto a greased pastry tray and score the pastry into squares of approx. ¼ inch.

Place in the oven and bake until the pastry is really hard.

Remove and allow to cool completely before breaking into small pieces.

When cool tip the biscuit into a plastic bag and hit with a rolling pin to break up the mixer.

Store the mixer biscuit in an airtight container until needed.

Liver Lumps

Training your puppy will be easier if you have some interesting and smelly treats to tempt him into performing. This and the following recipe are two of my favourites. Make the pieces as small as possible so that puppy only has a small morsel and not a meal.

Ingredients
450g raw pigs' liver
1 egg
1mug flour
1 teaspoon garlic granules

One greased baking tray

To make
Preheat oven to 200°C, Gas Mark 6

Blend the liver until it resembles a paste.

Add the other ingredients and mix well.

With floured fingers make small balls of the mix and place on the baking tray so that they do not touch.

Bake for 20 minutes for soft treats and longer for a hard chew. Dust with more of the garlic granules for added flavour.

Note: Very small liver lumps baked almost solid make delicious training aids.

For chew strips roll long strips of the mix in your hands and place on the tray to bake.

Peanut Marbles

These easy-to-make treats can be used when training your dog as they just love the flavour of peanut butter and will do anything for a taste. Keep the marbles small so that your dog stays slim.

Ingredients
3 mugs of wholemeal flour
2 tablespoons of baking powder
1 small jar of crunchy peanut butter
1 mug of milk

To make
Preheat the oven to 220°C, Gas Mark 7

Mix the flour and baking powder in a large mixing bowl.

In another bowl place the peanut butter and milk and mix together until they are combined.

Add the liquid mix to the flour and stir well. This should give you a firm dough-type mix.

Pull very small pieces from the dough and roll between your palms to form small balls.

Place each ball onto a greased baking tray and push the centre of each ball with your finger so that they are slightly flattened.

Bake in the centre of the oven until brown and firm and turn out onto a cooling tray.

When cold store in an airtight container.

The author's thoughts

I feel quite strongly that we should attempt to feed our dogs a home-made diet. Going back to basics when cooking for our family should include the dog when cooking with fresh ingredients. My book, *Canine Cuisine* (How To Books) shows how this can be done quite easily.

6

Children and Dogs

Sadly we read such horror stories in the press about dog attacks on children. Please be aware that it is only a miniscule number of dogs that do attack like this and quite often they are provoked into doing so through being teased, through stress due to the confines of their environment or through bad treatment and lack of training by the owner. Very few dogs would look at a human (of any age) and just leap at them intent on doing harm.

A dog can be enjoyed by all members of the family. The elderly have a purpose in life when there is a dog in the home. Routines have to be adhered to for the animal and interaction with a pet can get them out of the house and enjoying life rather than sitting at home and vegetating.

A dog can bring a family together, enjoying trips to the park and long walks in the countryside. Canine events shared with the whole family mean making plans to spend time together and looking forward to the weekend as a family pursuing joint activities rather than solitary hobbies.

SUPERVISION

A dog should never be left alone with a child of any age. Even if your dog is trained to a high level in obedience and has a temperament that is as solid as a rock someone should be there to supervise younger members of the family with your dog.

Accidents happen, tails can be trodden on, toys can startle a dog and he will by nature retaliate. Would you lie down and behave if a toddler poked you in the eye? I suspect I would most likely bite back, and so would a puppy who knows no different. If you watch a puppy playing with his siblings, they rough and tumble and they do nip. The mother of the puppies keeps her brood in order at all times and this can be with a growl or with dominance. The family dog will see the children either as his siblings or as his children and if play becomes rough or out of hand he will step in to control the situation or indeed join in. To humans this can be seen as aggression when it is simply a dog's way of controlling a situation and acting as a dog should. For a young child to be part of rough play with a dog or in a position where a dog is acting in a dominating way is not acceptable.

So, if you need to leave the room for even a minute pop the dog into his crate or take the child (or dog) with you. A second or two of common sense could avoid a lifetime of regret.

DOWN TIME

Every dog needs its own space, somewhere to sleep off a meal or get away from a lively young family. If you don't have a separate room with a baby gate to separate children and family a crate (or cage) may be the answer. A puppy that is introduced to a cage at an early age will see it as his room, his space where he can chill out, possibly eat his meals and also sleep at night. I have a twelve-year-old who loves his cage and refuses to eat elsewhere. We recently decided that he should sleep with his sisters as he had trouble getting to his feet first thing in the morning due to age-related stiffness in his hind leg. He thought differently and sulked like a teenager until we unlocked the door of the cage and let him in. He constantly nudged our legs, head butted us and nodded towards the cage as if to say, 'Open the door and let me in'. Once in the cage he turned his back on us to show he was not amused with our change to his routine. To get round this new problem we left him with a biscuit on his rugs and within days he was happy to sleep outside of the cage which has since been dismantled.

THE ALPHA OWNER

If you watch dogs in a pack, there is always a lead dog, the boss, the alpha dog. If you have several dogs there is always one that the others will defer to. In my home it has always been a bitch that is alpha dog. When we have suffered bereavement with our dogs it has been interesting to see who takes over and always it was the eldest daughter. In your home the adult should be the alpha leader. A dog should never be allowed to even think he is the boss of the household. Simple training from the first day puppy comes home with you should put you as the alpha person in the pack and the dog further down the pecking order.

A daily routine whereby your dog walks on lead and you are in control at playtime will see the dog quickly respect that you are the boss. Your children can be taught the same routines by working with the dog to sit and lie down on command and walking to heel when on a lead. Even coming when called and being taught to wait for treats rather than grabbing from the giver's hand will teach the dog how to respect his owners and other members of his new pack.

DOG CLUBS

I cannot praise enough the dog training clubs that are available for owners. The whole family should take part. The job of training the new puppy should not be left to one adult. From puppy socialisation classes at the veterinary surgery, to obedience, ringcraft, agility or even dancing to music there are basic beginners' classes. If you only book one three-month session of training it will be enough to give you an idea of how to train a dog. The leaders at these groups have worked with dogs most of their lives and know them inside out. They will show you simple tricks that will have your dog doing as he is told rather than ruling the roost. If the whole family can take time out to attend a class and learn how to handle the dog it will lead to a stress-free life with a happy dog. It's not too much to ask of your family is it?

Freddie will be attending training classes. It is important for him to learn how to mix with other dogs and for us to know how to work with him to be a good, well-behaved dog.

Sarah Alpe

OFF LEAD AND EXERCISE

Walking the dog is a daily event that should never be left to a child to do alone. Apart from stranger danger a child cannot react in the right way should a loose dog appear, or if your own dog runs away or into the road and causes an accident. However, taking the dog to an area where it can be let off lead and allowed to run is an ideal time for the child to learn how to control the family pet.

If a dog is likely to run away rather than come back when called use a long line (an old washing line will do) and attach one end to the dog's collar. Let the dog run loose but then call him back with a gentle tug of the long lead. A small treat in the hand will entice the dog back but only hand the treat over when the dog has sat down, not when he has jumped all over you in an exuberant fashion. If puppy ignores your call, a firm jerk on the lead (not one that will pull him over though) will remind him that you are in control. If this does not work go back to a shorter lead and start again.

Extend the lead a little more each time so that the dog goes further away. The saying, practice makes perfect is certainly true in this exercise. When your puppy has learned the tricks of coming when called practise the exercise off lead. Show him the treat in your hand before you start this to reinforce the fact he will be rewarded if he is good. NEVER give treats on demand and never reward the puppy if he has not performed as requested. Praise the puppy each time he is good and gradually withdraw the treats each time so that eventually your praise is enough to keep him happy.

Recalling your dog will take weeks of training as not many puppies will get the hang of it in a few days. Dogs want to please their family and will respond to praise. This is a training exercise that the younger members of the family can practise when out with their parents and the puppy. This is also something that can be practised in the garden when the puppy is still quite young.

HYGIENE

Young children love their dogs and will play with them quite happily. Puppies will lick and 'kiss' their owners, they will take food from their hands and play with toys. Young children need to be taught that dogs carry germs and that hands should be washed after playing with a dog and before they eat.

Children are never too young to learn how to pick up after a dog and to use a cloth to wipe up any accidents. Puppies are not toys and if children are to have the fun of a pet they should know about the hygienic side of pet care. When it comes to a puppy's meal time let the child help prepare the food and place the bowl on the floor. Let them learn how to wash the bowl afterwards with the cleaning cloths that are used for the puppy alone.

A child can also learn that a dog always needs a bowl of fresh clean water. It is a simple but essential task that they can take on as their job.

Picking up after a dog should be done by all the family and straight after it is deposited in the garden by your dog. Dog mess attracts flies and will smell very unpleasant. Left to rot it will upset your neighbours and you will be visited by the

environmental health inspectors who will fine you for your
unacceptable behaviour.

After picking up your dog's mess wash the area with a pleasant
disinfectant. Use one designed as a dog deodoriser that will
eliminate doggy smells and is dog friendly. If you use a non-doggy
brand check that the ingredients are not harmful to animals. A
child can help with washing the garden area used by your puppy
using a small-sized watering can, a capful of the disinfectant and
the garden water butt. Train your child in canine hygiene while
training your puppy!

TOYS

A dog should have its own toys and not chew and destroy those
belonging to the children in the family. Breaking a child's toys
will soon alienate the dog and the two will never bond.

If money is tight buy soft toys from jumble sales or allow the
puppy to have ones that the family no longer want. Remove any
hard objects such as plastic eyes and nose before giving to the
puppy to play with. These toys should be machine washable so
take care to check what filling is used as sometimes beans and
pulses are used as fillings.

Puppies love noisy toys and there is nothing noisier than an empty
plastic milk carton. Rinsed out and with the lid removed a puppy
can throw it around or race from room to room enjoying the
sound of the plastic cracking in his mouth. The cartons should not
damage furniture and can be replaced daily before little sharp
teeth start to rip it apart.

A toy that is ideal to leave a pet alone with if the family need to go out and leave him is a Kong. These are solid plastic shapes with holes in. The holes are packed with tasty food such as peanut butter that a little tongue needs to poke and prod to remove. Kongs come in all shapes and sizes to fit any breed of dog. They are washable and a godsend. I wouldn't be without one – or two!

Tasty bones are another favourite for most dogs. Use only raw bones as cooked bones can splinter and lodge in the throat. These will be carried around by puppies and chewed with gusto. Throw them away when they become dirty and smelly as they attract flies in the home during hot spells.

I'm not a fan of any form of hide chews and pigs ears. Some puppies swallow them causing blockages in the stomach which left unchecked can kill a dog. Always supervise a dog that is given a hide chew.

Freddie has a Good Boy teething bone which he can settle down with and chew. It is not only keeping his little teeth clean but distracts him from chewing the furniture.

Sarah Alpe

Dogs should always be happy for children and adults to take away their toys and food. A dog that growls and becomes aggressive when anyone gets close to their possessions needs to learn who is the boss, or alpha owner, as discussed at the beginning of this chapter.

The author's thoughts

My thoughts are that very young children and puppies should not mix.
So much so that I have never sold a puppy to a family with a child under
the age of five. I breed large dogs so to me it is a big concern; perhaps
breeders with smaller breeds have other opinions?

7

Canine Safety

Sadly, stories of lost and stolen dogs seem to be in the news most days. Some breeds are targeted for theft due to their exchange value on the streets for drugs and money. Stealing dogs for fighting is another fear we have to consider when owning some of the bull breeds.

Dogs can also become lost – it takes just a moment for them to go missing while off lead, or perhaps sneaking through a gap in the fence when they are let out into the garden and your back is turned. By securing your home and being aware when out walking your dog you can go some way to keeping your puppy safe.

MICROCHIPPING

At present the only identification your dog needs to have is an identification tag on his collar when outside the home. However, there are other more permanent ways to tag your dog. A microchip is the size of a grain of rice and is inserted under the skin between the shoulder blades of the dog. The chip contains a small electronic device with a unique number. When scanned by a hand device the number is picked up and checked against a log that shows that the dog belongs to you.

The hand-held scanners are used by police, vets, rescue centres and staff at all ports where animals pass through, as well as by private owners who like to ensure that their dogs' microchips are working correctly. Having a microchip inserted is one step towards being able to travel overseas and return into the UK without your dog having to go through six months of quarantine, as they did in the years before the pet passport was devised.

Puppies can be microchipped at a young age. This service is available from veterinary surgeries, charitable institutions such as The Dogs Trust and also through private business where staff are trained to undertake the insertion of the microchip. Anaesthetic is not needed and the process is no more painful than a vaccination.

AT HOME

♦ Are the fences in your back garden high enough to stop your dog jumping over them? What about underneath the fence? You would be surprised how easily some dogs can dig under a fence and make a bid for freedom.

- Garden gates should have a secure bolt on the inside to detract opportunist thieves from entering your property.

- Consider floodlighting your garden so that your dog can be outside and observed on the darkest evenings. Floodlights that switch on if someone walks into the proximity of your property are very appealing but can sometimes be triggered by cats and foxes. Solar powered lighting is a cheap way to light your garden.

- What about your front garden and gate, are they secure? Can your dog slip out of the front door and run into the road? Perhaps a safety chain on the door or a dog gate in the hall will stop his escape.

- Open windows can also offer a quick escape route to a young dog who hears an interesting noise or just fancies escaping to explore the outdoors. On the ground floor he will simply escape but on the first floor or higher his escape could prove fatal. Window locks that prevent children falling through open windows can also work for small pets. In fact many aids made for parents of toddlers come in very handy for owners of dogs.

OUT WALKING

When walking in built-up areas and near busy roads never be tempted to allow your dog off lead. Even the best behaved dog can trip someone up, run into the road or be taken from you. With a lead safely attached to your dog he can be hauled out of trouble in an instant. I'm very wary of the extendable leads. What if the retractable part does not work that quickly and your dog runs in the path of a car? Can you guarantee that the long length of the lead will not trip up another pedestrian? These are better kept for the park or garden when training your puppy.

If your dog walking takes place at night or in an area that you feel uncomfortable with why not organise for a group of local dog walkers to meet up and walk together? There is safety in crowds.

By all means allow children to learn to walk your puppy properly but never alone. Always have an adult with the child and dog. You may think this is a silly point but children can be mugged not just for their mobile phone and pocket money but for their dog as well.

LOOSE DOGS

Be aware of loose dogs when out with your dog. If they approach stand your ground and look for the owner of the dog. If you have a small dog by all means pick him up but if the approaching dog is aggressive he will be more inclined to jump up at a yapping dog in your arms. Keep cool and keep calm. Try to encourage your own dog to stay calm and quiet. Never run away as the loose dog will follow. Stand your ground, do not wave your arms or scream. Using a very deep voice use a one word command such as 'down' or 'leave'. Do not kick out as you could be bitten. Report the loose dog and the incident to the park warden, dog warden, local council and even the police if the attack was very aggressive.

LOCAL BY-LAWS

Remember that the owners of loose dogs are breaking the law by not having their dog under control. If your dog is not under control you could be the person facing a fine or, worse, you could be the owner of a dog that injures someone. Although local by-laws can change they do cover dogs that are out of control and also owners that do not clear up after their dog. Fines can be hefty.

Check what the dog laws are for your area. Most local councils have a detailed website but if in doubt write a letter and ask. Having a guideline in writing is better than a verbal response to any query concerning your dog.

It is your legal obligation to have your dog wear a collar and identification disc at all times when outside the home.

LOST AND STOLEN DOGS

Anyone who has had their dog disappear will remember that gut-wrenching moment they realised that their four-legged friend had vanished. The first instinct is to rush around screaming out the dog's name in terror wondering if he has run into the road or been stolen by people who want to exchange him for drugs or lead him into a life of dog fighting and abuse.

In these frightening minutes try to keep calm and follow these guidelines:

♦ Call for him but not in a high-pitched voice as this could make him more excitable and inclined to run in the wrong direction even more.

♦ Do not shout as he may think he has done something wrong and be less inclined to come back to you.

♦ Use keywords that have always attracted his attention – dinner and biccies does it in my house!

♦ If you are in a park or area that he knows follow footpaths that he will remember.

♦ Ask other walkers to look out for him.

♦ Always carry a mobile phone for such emergencies and have his photograph stored to show people as they may not know the breed of your dog.

♦ Ring home and check he has not headed that way. Ask family at home to start walking towards you just in case the dog is heading homewards.

♦ Also check the car park if you have driven to the park as dogs do love a car ride and will recognise their owner's vehicle.

Most times, when a dog goes missing he is simply having a good sniff around and has not run away or been stolen. He will be found within 15 minutes and apart from you needing a cup of tea and a sit down no harm has been done. However, if your dog does not appear you need to put a plan into action.

♦ Call family and friends to help in your search. Cover gardens, alleyways and roads that surround the area. Ponds, streams, lakes and rivers in the area should also be checked in case he is playing in water or has sadly got into difficulties.

♦ As the hours pass if your dog has not turned up you need to start to contact people who can help. Friends, family and neighbours are the obvious choice but your local church community, friends from the children's schools and any clubs that you belong to can also be called upon in times like this.

- ◆ Telephone the following people and if days pass and your dog is not found ring them every day just in case he has turned up:
  - *Your local police station*: Police no longer keep lost dogs, as this job is now undertaken by the local council and dog wardens, but many people do still take dogs to the police when they are found so it is worth speaking to them. Speak to your local community police officer as they patrol the area and may spot a loose dog. If you feel your dog was stolen make sure that this is noted and that you receive a crime number. It will help at a later date if you need help to recover your dog and may also be needed for insurance purposes.
  - *Veterinary surgeries and dog hospitals in the area*: If you've followed the guidelines below you will already have a list to work from.

- ◆ Start producing posters and hand them out in the area where your dog was last seen. Local shops, pet stores, notice boards, in fact everywhere. It is not unheard of for council workers to remove posters from lamp posts so keep refreshing them. To keep posters dry slip them into plastic sleeves with the opening at the bottom. When your dog is found remember to go round and remove the posters and thank the shops that helped.

Locating your dog may take weeks or even months. There has been news of dogs returning after many years. Keep yourself busy with your search, ringing dog-related businesses and keeping local people who may have knowledge of his whereabouts abreast of the situation. Groups like DogLost are there as a shoulder to cry on as well as a united group of dog lovers who will carry you through this distressful time.

Plan ahead

Posters

As silly as it seems, plan ahead just in case your dog should go missing. We all have access to a computer or know someone who is savvy enough to work one on our behalf.

Always keep up-to-date photographs of your dog on the computer. Several different angled shots of him are better than a thousand words of description. Here are the ideal photographs to have:

- A full face view looking square on to him.

- Left side of the head.

- Right side of the head – all three of these will show the head markings.

- The whole of your dog's left side while standing. Include the tail as sometimes they are docked or of an unusual length.

- An image of his right side.

- A photograph of the dog standing next to an adult, as this will give an overall image of his size.

- Images of any scars, unusual marks and tattoos (some dogs are tattooed for identity purposes).

Next, keep a list of his height, weight, colouring and any little habits he has.

With these details make up a poster leaving a space to show when and where he was lost and who to contact. Never give your address as some people will take advantage of you being out looking for your dog and burgle your home.

Be wary of offering a reward as there are instances of people tricking owners into paying more money or even passing off the wrong dog. Sadly, pedigree dogs are seen as a way to make money out of owners and it is not uncommon for dogs to be stolen for ransom.

With the basic information on a poster it will take no time at all to add some final details and have posters printed and ready to distribute in the unfortunate instance of your dog going missing. Hopefully it will never need to be used but it is a project that can be done in advance perhaps with the help of your children who will also learn about dog safety from this exercise.

Contact list

Have a list prepared of people who can help if your dog should go missing. Be prepared to ring these people daily – even twice daily if necessary.

♦ Vets: Make a list of all veterinary surgeries in a ten mile radius from your home. It's amazing how far dogs can walk and he may be handed in if he has been injured. Vets do scan dogs and this is the way you can be reunited with your dog if he has been microchipped or tattooed.

♦ Dog wardens in surrounding council areas: Also find out what kennels the dogs are placed into by the wardens as these may be private establishments. Ring direct to these kennels.

♦ Dog rescue centres. Dogs can be handed in directly by a member of the public.

♦ Pet shops: News of lost and found pets are often displayed at these stores so again research telephone numbers both to check if your dog is being shown as found and also to place a poster of your own.

♦ National and local lost dog organisations: These are marvellous organisations where dedicated people help the owners of lost dogs distribute posters and track down dogs. Many of these volunteers have themselves lost dogs and know what to do to help you. Most groups work with the media when searching for a dog; they also have a page dedicated to each dog and send out email bulletins to helpers in each area to alert them that a dog has gone missing in their patch. These organisations are a godsend to dog owners and most are run on a very tight budget.

Here are a few national groups, but do try to add local organisations to your list.

♦ DogLost
www.doglost.co.uk

♦ Alfie's Lost Dogs
www.alfieslostdogs.com

♦ Animal Search UK
www.animalsearchuk.co.uk

♦ Local newspapers: Although newspapers will not run news of every lost dog if there is a newsworthy hook they may help you. News on stolen dogs will always be run.

- Local radio stations are always pleased to pass on news of local pets that go missing.

- Facebook and Twitter are new ways of informing the world that your dog has been lost or stolen.

- Dogs have been known to stray onto railway lines with disastrous consequences. However, staff do try and reunite much-loved pets with their owners so find out the contact number for the railway maintenance people in your area.

- Dogs killed on roads are collected and disposed of sympathetically. Each council waste department has a team that collects animals so ask at your council depot for the contact number.

- Petlog
  This is the Kennel Club's own 24-hour pet recovery service. Join Petlog by registering your dog's unique microchip number and they will work with you if your dog should be lost or stolen by matching up your dog's microchip number with many of the organisations that are likely to have come across your dog.
  www.petlog.org.uk
  0844 4633 999

Pet Insurance

Check your policy as you may be covered for assistance whilst looking for your dog. Many policies also offer financial help if your dog should die.

At this point I should mention that there is a vast array of companies offering pet insurance. Check what is available and decide what you need cover for. Don't dismiss the policies offered by supermarkets and chain stores as they offer some of the best deals and at cheaper prices.

EVERYDAY DANGERS

Common foods

I have listed the most common foods below but if you are unsure of any foodstuff's effect on your dog leave it out of the recipe and make enquiries before it proves fatal. Mention dogs and toxic food and myths and urban legends start to be circulated. 'Carrots are killers' is my favourite. Well, yes they would be if you were stabbed through the heart with one but normally a raw carrot is a low calorie treat for a tubby dog and helps clean the teeth. Give it to a dog that has a tendency to swallow his food whole and it could possibly cause an obstruction – but then so could any food!

Alcohol

Some owners think it's a good joke to give their dogs beer or let them finish off the dregs from glasses after a party. First, dogs are much smaller than us and can get drunk much quicker on a lot less alcohol. They do not know about the effects felt when drunk so can become very frightened as their body is affected by the alcohol, they cannot walk or stand and are then very sick. What owners do not realise is that alcohol is toxic to a dog as after the similar effects felt by humans a dog can fall into a coma and die.

Avocado

The high fatty content of avocado can cause stomach problems, vomiting and in severe cases pancreatitis. Persin, which is found in the avocado, is toxic to a dog and can damage the heart and lungs. Furthermore the large stone found in the centre of an avocado can be swallowed by your pet and become lodged in the throat or intestines.

Caffeine

Drinks containing caffeine can contain theobromine or theophylline. This is toxic to a dog and can cause damage to the heart and nervous system.

Chocolate

A chemical called theobromide is fatal for dogs and as little as two ounces of chocolate with a high cocoa content can be fatal. The higher the cocoa content the higher the toxicity of the product. Consequently white chocolate is not as potent as a high quality dark chocolate. Sadly before a dog dies he will experience a great deal of pain, sickness and seizures. Even six ounces could be fatal to a dog of 20k. Seek medical attention at once should your dog ingest chocolate. When cooking with chocolate for dogs use carob or doggy choc drops.

Please note: Bark chippings in your garden could possibly be cocoa bark which is toxic to a dog. Ask at your garden centre before purchasing such a product.

Cooked bones

Cooked bones should never be given to a dog. Cooking softens the bone and it will splinter, pierce internal organs and cause fatality. A raw meaty bone is much more beneficial to a dog.

Corn cobs

It is so tempting to throw the corn cob to your dog after eating the fleshy sweet corn yourself. The cob can cause internal obstructions or choke the dog if they swallow large pieces.

Fruit pips and stones

Pips or stones from apples, cherries, peaches, plums, pears, apricots, etc. contain cyanide which is fatal to a dog. Fruit stones can also choke a dog or become lodged internally and cause great pain to our pets and possibly even death.

Garlic

There seems to be a great debate about the toxicity of garlic and its affect on dogs. Garlic is a natural cleanser and works well in our battle against fleas. It is the overuse of garlic that can cause a problem. By overuse we are talking of in excess of one bulb for a dog and we are never going to add that much to our dog's dinner are we? Garlic capsules are available for dogs from some of the top pet retailers in the UK (see the products list at the end of the book) and I have used them for many years with no ill effects on my dogs.

Grapes and raisins

These can cause serious damage to a dog's kidneys – fatal, in fact. It is so easy to throw a few to a begging dog so please stop and think before sharing such foods.

Macadamia nuts

While not fatal, these can cause serious illness.

Onions

Onion can be the cause of anaemia in dogs. Be careful when feeding ready-made meals meant for babies or adults as they may include large amounts of onion. A small quantity can be used for flavouring a recipe.

Sweeteners

Sugar-free sweeteners that contain Xylitol can cause serious illness in a dog. Check the ingredient listing carefully when purchasing such products.

Tomatoes

This surprised me as my dogs have often had a slice of tomato from my plate or while I've been cooking. While researching this book the question of tomatoes being toxic kept popping up on canine forums, but you can be safely assured that tomatoes will not affect your dog.

Yeast dough

Yeast dough has a rising agent in it that has not been killed off by heat while baking. Consequently the dough could continue to ferment internally and cause wind, pain and possibly rupturing of internal organs. Small pieces of cooked bread are fine to feed your dog as long as it does not replace a meal but there are better foods for your pet. Why not try raw vegetables?

Plants in the garden

Cala lilies, foxglove, crocus, narcissus and peonies in the garden, for example, are very toxic to pets and can kill. Others can cause mouth irritation and serious illness.

Try to keep your puppy away from the planted area of the garden. Not only will dogs trample and destroy valued flowers and plants but they will snuffle around in the earth and nibble at interesting discoveries. Once ingested these new discoveries can cause upset tummies and worse. Bulbs can be dug up by inquisitive puppies and eaten with delight – dogs know no better! Keep an eye on your dog while enjoying your garden and check which plants are best kept out of harm's way.

Check any products used in your garden to control pests. Slug pellets and sprays can be lethal to dogs. In fact why not stop using any type of product in your garden and go down the natural organic route to gardening?

Organic gardening may be the way ahead for dog owners who are worried about their dogs making contact with harmful products. Remember though that whatever way you garden some of the plants you grow can kill your beloved pet.

The author's thoughts

The safety of a pet is as important as the safety of your children. I've worked with people looking for their lost dogs and the stories and the heartbreak are horrendous. Never knowing where the dog has gone, wondering if it is being cared for or has faced an awful death. We all hope our dogs will stay safe. By taking precautions and knowing what to do if something does happen we can be prepared for the worst eventuality.

8

Travelling with a puppy

A puppy's first encounter with a car is likely to be when he is brought home for the first time. No doubt he will have been swaddled in blankets and held by one of the family so would have been unaware of the journey. A dog who joins a car-owning family needs to become used to car travel as there are going to be times he needs to travel to the vet and other places that are important in his little life.

FROM DAY ONE

Even though a puppy cannot interact with other dogs or walk in public places until he has completed his vaccinations he can travel in your car. It may be too much to place him into a cage or tether him to a seat belt but there is no reason he cannot sit on the back seat with another member of the family and get used to the motion of the vehicle. Start with short journeys until car travel is second nature to your dog. A cover for the seats would be a good idea as an excited puppy can have an accident. Wet wipes and kitchen paper make ideal cleaning equipment to leave in the car. Wet wipes can also be used to wipe down dog marks left on upholstery and leave behind a pleasant smell.

Once longer journeys are undertaken plan to stop at least every hour so that puppy can stretch his legs and have a drink and a wee.

CAR EQUIPMENT

Dogs, like small children, should never travel in a car on the front seat. Although there is not yet legislation about pets travelling in cars it is common sense to ensure that the animal is safe during the journey. If you are a lone driver and the dog becomes upset he can cause an accident by taking your mind away from the road if he is misbehaving or jumping all over the place like a lunatic. I've seen it happen. You've no doubt seen the television advertisements where back seat passengers become missiles and can kill themselves as well as others if there was an accident? The same can happen with a loose dog in the car. A dog needs to be restrained for his own safety and the safety of the other passengers.

I have both a separate crate and plastic travelling box. I disapprove of dog safety belts and harnesses. I consider them dangerous.

Anthony Milton

Cages and bars

It is possible to purchase a bespoke cage that fits into the back of a car and is designed to match the shape of the model of your car. Some manufacturers sell them as one of the many accessories available to new car buyers. There are also companies that make the cages to order. Advertisements for these companies can be found in canine publications such as *Our Dogs* and *Your Dog*.

The cage should be fixed firmly to the vehicle so that in an accident or shunt the dog and cage do not move. Some models have been known to withstand a car rolling and the dog has walked away from the accident. Escape doors in two places will mean that a dog can be removed with ease. These cages are very much like the cage or crate used in the home. Some have partitions so that several dogs can travel separately and in safety.

Dog bars that stretch to fit behind the back seat in an estate car are ideal if they can be fixed to the body of the vehicle. They need to withstand a lively large dog or the dog and bars could tumble down onto the back seat passengers.

> *We have always kept our dogs on leads when out in public and they are safe in the car with seat belts. I have knowledge of canine first aid and have a first aid kit in the car for emergencies.*
>
> June Crowe

Seat belts

There are some fantastic seat belts for dogs on the market. Years ago my dogs could escape these contraptions with ease but these days they are well designed and even come padded so they are comfortable for any shape of dog. Fitted like a body harness there is a clip that fits onto the seat belt and can be released in exactly the same way as a seat belt worn by a passenger. An additional clasp means that many of the harnesses can be clipped to the dog's lead ready to walk from the car.

Seat covers

Manufacturers of canine equipment have come up with some great gear for our cars. Waterproof covers for car seats are a great idea. These can be found advertised on eBay and in canine publications. They are washable and can be fitted easily or removed when human passengers are on board. Old towels are ideal to place on the seats as they can be washed when muddy and also used to dry a wet dog.

Collars and leads

Even the owner of a small puppy must obey the law regarding taking a dog outside the home. **The control of dogs order (1992)** states that any dog in a public place must wear a collar and tag with the owner's name and address. A telephone number is optional. My dogs' tags have the name of the dog on one side and my surname, address and landline number on the other. Rather than name your street simply show your house number and postcode – that way if the tag is read by a stranger your empty home is not at risk. Make sure his collar has a disc with your name and phone number just in case he runs away. Always take off the lead when a dog is travelling in the vehicle as it may get caught on something and cause an injury to the dog. I always keep several dog leads in the car just in case we lose one or if we come across a loose dog. We prefer the soft nylon ones that can be washed. These are handy when dogs have been in the mud or on the beach.

Bus and train
There may be times when you have to use public transport with your dog. Be prepared to pay for a ticket and do not let your dog sit on the seats. Check ahead of your journey as some bus companies do not allow dogs on their vehicles.

Food and water
There is no need to have food for the dog to eat while actually travelling. Not only will it make a mess but a young dog could choke or be sick. Pack dog biscuits for a long journey and have a bottle of water ready for stops. Most pet stores sell non-splash water bowls or collapsible bowls for travelling.

Contact details
Keep a card in the car that states there is a dog on board. If you have an accident and are unable to speak to the rescue services they will be aware that a dog was with you and may have escaped from the damaged vehicle. The same should be done with dogs left at home. Have a contact number visible of a key holder to your home who can get into the house to care for your dogs.

Hot dogs
Never be tempted to leave a dog in the car even for a few minutes. The temperature in a car can rise dramatically and leaving the

window open a few inches will not help the dog trapped inside. Take your dog with you but if that is not possible leave him at home or place him in boarding kennels.

BOARDING KENNELS

If you intend to holiday without your dog he will need to be taken care of. Friends and family may be happy to take him in for a few days but consider whether he will be a burden to them or will pine for his family and drive his foster carers to distraction with his distress. There are organisations that will house- and pet-sit and I am informed the people are reliable and security checked. However, for the majority of us a boarding kennel is the only option.

Never leave booking into a kennel until the last minute as the good ones are booked far ahead of the holiday season. If you are new to the area and have no knowledge of the best kennels speak to your vet and friends who have dogs as they will be able to recommend good kennels and point out the not so good ones. Make an appointment to visit the boarding kennel to see if your dog will be happy there.

A good kennel will feed your dog his preferred menu, walk him each day and spend time with him so he is not lonely. The kennel will have a vet on call and be able to offer extra services such as grooming and bathing.

Your dog's vaccinations will have to be up to date and documentation will need to be shown when he is taken for his canine holiday. If your dog is not covered for kennel cough ask your vet for the relevant cover just in case he catches the illness while in the kennels.

HOLIDAYS

Many dogs enjoy holidays with their owners each year. When you intend to take your dog with you make sure that the hotel, campsite, guest house or rented cottage accepts dogs. Usually up to two well-behaved dogs are accepted and there may be a small charge.

Take a few old sheets with you to cover furnishing and the bed. Take care that the holiday rental does not smell doggy and that you do not leave pet hairs behind afterwards. Leaving a holiday rental clean and smelling sweet will mean you can book to return another year.

When travelling to a holiday destination check out Travelodge motels for overnight stays, as they accept well-behaved, clean dogs (www.travelodge.co.uk).

I will be taking Matilda away on holiday as often as I can. I regularly rent a Kentish seaside cottage where dogs are welcome.

Kelly Rose Bradford

Eating out

Eating out when you have a dog can cause problems. Restaurants and cafes do not as a rule accept our four-legged friends. When planning a holiday check online for pubs and restaurants. There are many eating places listed with gardens and outside dining areas where dogs are welcome. Family picnics are another option and can be enjoyed at any picnic spot or beach. Open for Dogs gives a list of dog friendly places to stay and eat: www. kcdogfriendly.co.uk

Beaches

Sadly many beaches are out of bounds to dogs from May until the end of September each year. Rather than find yourself with a hefty fine for stepping onto a beach in the wrong part of the season look at the information distributed by tourist information centres to see when your dog is welcome.

Why not take your holiday in a month when you and your dog are welcome or better still spend your money in a seaside resort that is more welcoming to a family with a dog?

Stately homes and tourist spots

Dogs are not always welcome in tourist spots although they may have a designated dog car park where there is shade and a tap for fresh water. Do not be fooled into thinking this is good enough for your dog. Any length of time he is left in a car can cause problems. Even in a shaded spot a car can get hot and a dog can die.

Countryside code

Always follow the country code. Keep your dog on a lead in fields where there are farm animals and close all gates. Keep to footpaths and pick up after your dog at all times. If there isn't a bin to deposit your dog waste then carry it with you until you do find a bin. Do not be part of the new craze to leave the bag hanging from a tree. The bags simply rot and the dog waste drops to the ground to make more mess.

PET PASSPORT

With the introduction of the Pet Travel Scheme (pet passport) there is now the chance to take your dog overseas to many of the world's destinations. Your dog can travel by air as cargo or in your car via many of the UK's ports. The passport rules are to protect the pets and livestock in our country and as such cover your re-entry into the UK not your departure.

It can take over six months to organise a pet passport so take note of what you have to do and follow it to the letter. Make a mistake and your dog could end up spending six months in quarantine when he returns to the UK, which is very costly and upsetting for the whole family as well as your dog.

The Department for the Environment, Food and Rural Affairs (DEFRA) governs the pet passport and sets the rules for pet travel. At this time only dogs, cats and ferrets have the need for the passport.

Dogs from other countries have to conform to the pet passport scheme before they can visit the UK.

What to do
1. Your dog needs to be microchipped and the chip has to work when scanned.

2. Your dog must be vaccinated against rabies. The details are recorded by your vet on official paperwork. This must be done after the dog has been microchipped.

3. Rabies booster injections must be updated when due and recorded on your pet's documents.

4. Blood tests have to be done to check that the rabies vaccination has 'taken'. This has to be done by an EU-approved laboratory. Your vet can take you through this procedure and organise your pet passport.

5. You may travel overseas as soon as the passport has been received. However, your dog cannot return to the UK until six months after the results of the blood test show that the rabies vaccination has worked.

6. When re-entering the UK your dog must be treated for ticks and tapeworm. This has to be done not less than 24 hours and no more than 48 hours of reaching the point of entry.

Your dog has to be treated with a reputable product against the worm *Echinococcus multilocularis* before returning to the UK. Your vet can supply you with details of overseas contacts who are able to provide this service.

For further information and updates on countries taking part in the pet travel scheme visit the DEFRA website: www2.defra.gov. uk/wildlife-pets/pets/travel

The author's thoughts

I prefer to holiday with my dogs rather than leave them in kennels, but as they have grown older has not always been possible. Short trips to the coast and to visit parks and countryside are enjoyed by my dogs who then go home to a bed that they know.

9

Hobbies with your dog

There are so many things that a family can do to enjoy the company of their dog. Apart from walks and holidays there are many canine sports to consider, as well as charity work. The choice is yours and whatever you choose is open to all the family to join in with from the very young to the retired person with time on their hands.

Here is a selection of canine hobbies, but there are many more to choose from.

AGILITY

This is a fast and enjoyable sport and can be played at competition level as well as for fun. You and your dog would have to be fairly fit as you have to run beside your dog as he attempts to jump, tunnel and balance on obstacles. Winners are found by timed trials and penalties are given for wrong routes around the course. The course is set out depending on the level of competence as well as the size of the dog. Agility clubs do have taster days and beginners' classes.

DOG SHOWING

This is not just a beauty show as all dogs exhibited have to be fit for purpose. Young and old can show their dogs at Kennel Club registered events and there are small shows (called Open Shows) and larger championship shows to attend. Breed clubs also have individual breed shows for beginners as well as champion dogs and their owners. These shows are worth visiting to watch dogs and to meet owners and breeders when you are first picking out a suitable breed for your family. Dogs have to qualify by winning a major class at a championship show in order to compete at Crufts each year. My book, *Showing Your Dog: A Beginner's Guide* gives step-by-step information about enjoying this delightful sport.

FLYBALL

Flyball is another fast action-packed sport for dogs, although the owners do not have to run with them. Teams of dogs race over small hurdles to a box at the end of the course where they release a ball (the size of a tennis ball) and race back to their owner where the next dog in the team takes over in the form of a relay race. Like other dog sports there are beginners' classes as well as advanced classes and the sport is open to any fit dog. For details of flyball clubs in your area contact The British Flyball Association: www.flyball.org.uk

FUN DOG SHOWS

These are known as Companion Shows and are run under licence from the Kennel Club. Any dog can enter these shows as there are classes for pedigree dogs as well as non-pedigree dogs. Entries are taken on the day and registration documents are not required for entry. These dog shows are held to raise money for charities and prizes and rosettes are donated for the winners. Entry only costs a few pounds and usually sideshows and refreshments are laid on to make the day a proper family event. Children are encouraged to handle their dogs in the ring. Special classes are held for dogs rehomed through rescue associations. Look in your local newspaper for details of fun dog shows in your area or read *Our Dogs* (the weekly paper for the canine world) for details of all types of dog shows.

HEELWORK TO MUSIC

Anyone who watches the last night of Crufts on the television cannot fail to be amazed by Mary Rae as she dances to show tunes with her dogs. As the dogs follow her steps and keep in time to the music weaving and prancing around her I'm sure we all wonder if our dogs could do the same.

Heelwork to music came into fashion in the dog world following on from set heelwork exercises in obedience competitions. These days young and old alike are dancing to country and western or bopping to the latest pop tunes along with their four-legged friends. Although there are competitions in this new sport the classes can also be a way to exercise yourself as well as your dog or just go out and have a fun time.

JUNIOR HANDLING

Any child can work with his or her dog but there is a special section of the Kennel Club for younger dog lovers. Called the Young Kennel Club it caters for all those between the ages of 6 and 24. Those in all aspects of dog sports are keen to invest in the future of dogdom and that means our children need to be encouraged not only to look after their dogs but to follow dog-based hobbies as well.

Watching any young person working with a dog or competing in the show ring shows how much the Kennel Club has worked to make the Young Kennel Club a success. With workshops, training camps and online activities there is something for every young person even if they do not yet own a dog. You can find out more on their website: www.ykc.org.uk

OBEDIENCE TRAINING

Every dog and owner should attend a class and basic obedience is the one to choose. Don't think that because your dog is a pet he doesn't need to know how to behave. For the cost of a few pounds each week you will learn simple tricks that will have your dog becoming obedient and a model citizen. If obedience training really grabs you continue to the higher classes and think about competing. It's a great sport that all the family can enjoy.

Walking to heel, sit stays, off lead stays and recalls are just some of the skills your dog can learn as well as working alongside other dogs and handlers and having a good time.

Talking of your dog becoming a model citizen did you know that there are Good Citizen tests for our dogs? This is the largest dog training scheme in the UK and anyone can join in and take the basic bronze test, and then work on to the higher silver and gold awards. Details of the Good Citizen Awards and classes are available at dog training classes or from the Kennel Club: www.thekennelclub.org.uk/dogtraining

KENNEL CLUB

The Kennel Club has a long list of registered clubs and groups that offer every kind of dog sport and interest throughout the UK: www.thekennelclub.org.uk/services/public/club/activity

CHARITY WORK AND VOLUNTEERING

There are ways that you can work with your dog either to raise money for charity or work with a charity.

Become a dog walker with The Guide Dog Association, the Cinnamon Trust or take your dog to visit the elderly or those in hospital with Pets As Therapy (PAT dogs). Helping out at canine rescue centres can also be very rewarding and there is bound to be such a centre close to your home. You may even be able to offer short-term fostering to a dog needing a home.

Even for people who cannot have a dog at home there are ways to work with our four-legged friends and help those less fortunate than ourselves.

Here are just a few of the many organisations that would love help from you if you can spare a few hours each week:

Guide Dogs
www.guidedogs.org.uk/helpus/volunteering/

The Cinnamon Trust
www.cinnamon.org.uk/volunteers.html

Pets As Therapy (PAT)
www.petsastherapy.org/

Battersea Dogs and Cats Home
www.battersea.org.uk/get_involved/volunteer_with_us/

Dogs Trust
www.dogstrust.org.uk/az/v/volunteerfostercarers/

If you have a favourite breed there are breed rescue centres for many of these lovely dogs. Ask through one of the breed clubs about their rescue schemes. Even if you cannot help at the kennels you may become a valued fundraiser or advisor and become part of the hard-working group of dog lovers that help the many wonderful dogs find their 'forever homes'.

The author's thoughts

Owning a dog means more than keeping him at home and taking a daily walk. So much can be enjoyed by a family who experience canine hobbies and sports.

10

The years ahead

Bringing home a puppy is an exciting time; you will have planned ahead, purchasing toys, bedding and food that he will enjoy. It may be that the family have had to change their work or holiday arrangements to accommodate a dog and life will have settled into a new routine. In the years to come your life and family commitments are sure to change and this is when you should still be considering your dog and his life as part of the family.

THE ADOLESCENT DOG

As your dog gets older he will grow, need more food, more exercise and probably more attention. This is where your research into the best dog for your family will pay off. You will know what to expect, will belong to dog clubs and have contacts in the breed and know where to go to gain advice with any problems with your growing dog. Keep in touch with the breeder as he or she will have the knowledge of living with a growing dog and can guide you through his adolescence.

This is the time when any dominance issues will surface. If you did not attend dog training classes it is not too late to start. A firm hand now will turn your dog back into the family friend and not a dog to be afraid of. A vet cannot prescribe a pill to cure an unruly dog and castration in males does not really stop naughtiness. Paying a behaviourist to sort out your dog may be the answer but it costs big bucks and to be honest it is your problem to solve not someone else's. A good obedience class can have you and your dog back on track in no time. Sending a dog off to be trained by a behaviourist or obedience expert does not work unless the family are trained at the same time.

Your dog's diet may have changed over the years and new concepts in feeding will arrive. If you want to change your dog's diet remember to do it over several weeks to avoid tummy upsets. Watch your dog to see that he is thriving on his new food and is not losing or putting on weight.

Continue to visit your vet for a yearly check up on your dog even if you no longer have booster vaccinations. Many people do stop boosters and any vet will run a blood check to see if an older dog has built up immunity and no longer needs the drugs. The yearly health checks will show if there are any health issues appearing and will give you peace of mind that your dog is happy and healthy.

BREEDING

Never consider breeding from your dog to make money. Any good dog breeder will tell you that the time spent caring for the bitch and the puppies is not cost effective and is a labour of love rather than labouring for cash. Ask yourself why you want to breed a litter. If it is to keep a puppy yourself and to breed healthy happy dogs for others to own then go ahead, but research all that breeding entails before you take your bitch to the stud dog.

Has your own dog been screened for every health concern for your breed? If you do not know what these are speak to your dog's own breeder or contact a breed club. If you have left it too late to screen your dog or find he or she is not quite the perfect example of the breed you imagined them to be why not buy another puppy and enjoy that rather than breed less than perfect puppies?

Take advice from more experienced owners of the breed when picking a stud dog. Although close breeding (mother to son, sister to brother) should be avoided there is something to be said for keeping your breeding to certain lines in your dog's pedigree. Experienced breeders within your chosen breed can teach you a lot about breeding a dog so hang on to their words and remember what you are told.

You will be responsible for every puppy that you breed. Keep in touch with them and their owners for the length of the dog's life and share the owner's joy with owning a beautiful dog that you brought into this life and also shed a tear with them when that life comes to an end.

We always have a questionnaire and a home visit before selling one of our puppies and I undertake all health screening for the breed. I will say no to someone if I feel that they are unsuitable candidates to own one of my dogs. I'm prepared to take back a dog if it cannot stay with its family.

Janet Swannell

THE OLDER DOG

Living with an elderly dog is a joy. It may be that your dog can no longer walk as far and may be a little stiff in the morning. You will find yourself working around your dog's needs, even his demands as the older dog can rule the roost in any home – albeit it in a good way. He will have learned little tricks over the years and become quite stubborn if his routine is changed or if you forget to give him his bedtime biscuit.

Eyes become dim and hearing more muffled; his teeth may no longer be able to chomp on a crunchy treat or bone. Your dog will still enjoy his meals but may not be able to eat a large bowl of food. Return to feeding your dog two or three smaller meals each day and have the door open so he can go straight outside and do his business. Accidents will happen as some dogs do become a little incontinent, but work with your dog to make his slide into old age as happy and carefree as possible.

An extra thick rug to sleep on at night, a light left on so he can see his way around – little considerations for your old friend will make his life easier.

Your dog may not be able to walk as far but he will still enjoy a car ride so do not take away all his joys in life. A waterproof cover on the car seat and a trip out with his family will mean he can enjoy your company and not be confined to the home day after day.

MARRIAGE BREAK UP

When a marriage fails and a couple splits there are many considerations such as who will have the children, where you will live and how you will cope. These may all be at the top of the list, but your dog must be considered to. A dog will have been accustomed to a routine in the home; he will know his family and will be upset if any member of his family suddenly vanishes from his life. The break-up of the family can affect a dog and he can suffer from stress very much as we can. He may revert to puppy behaviour, chewing and damaging the furniture. He may also start to bark and howl if left alone, as he does not understand that you are coming home and may feel he is losing another member of his family.

Decisions must to be made as to who will have your dog – perhaps you could both share him. I know of instances where this has been done with great success and the dogs are happy to be handed over to their mum or dad each weekend. They will have two sets of parents and two homes plus twice the love they had before.

NO MONEY

Redundancy and the recession have had a major impact on all dog rescue groups as thousands more dogs go into kennels or are put to sleep. Try to plan for your dog to stay with the family if you can, perhaps by feeding cheaper food or even selling personal belongings to fund his keep. The major canine charities have schemes whereby free or reduced price vaccinations and other essential canine care can be found. The PDSA provides a remarkable service covering the health care of dogs and other pets belonging to owners on benefits or in reduced circumstances. In areas that the PDSA does not cover there is help available from the RSPCA. When signing on at the job centre and claiming for benefits ask about help with pet care as there could be a leaflet with help and advice. Use the library and the citizen's advice centre to collect information on help available for owners of pets. There is a list of useful contact details at the end of this book, but you can find out more about the PDSA at www.pdsa.org.uk/pdsa-vet-care

If I needed to rehome my dog I couldn't go back to the breeder as she no longer breeds dogs. I would probably go through my vet as I trust him completely. I did this when I had a cat with a fractured pelvis who needed a home outdoors in a shedded area that we had no space for. He found a fantastic home and they kept me up to date with the cat's welfare for many years.

Dawn Hudd

YOUR DOG'S BREEDER

If there is no possibility that your dog can live with you go back to his breeder. Even if you have lost contact he or she will be happy to help you. A breeder's commitment is for the life of the dog and does not stop when you hand over your hard-earned cash and walk out of the door with the puppy. The breeder may not necessarily be able to take the dog into her home but she can help you find a new home where he will be loved and welcomed for the rest of his life.

Your breeder may have moved in which case go to the Kennel Club for help in locating them. As a registered breeder or an accredited breeder their name may be on a list.

BREED CLUBS

If you still have had no luck in contacting your dog's breeder go to the breed club as they will have knowledge of the breeder and where she now lives. Breed clubs also have a rehoming service where they help an owner find a new home for their dog, or failing that they will guide you to their rescue service. Breed rescue is run by dedicated volunteers who will make sure that your dog is well cared for in a kennel or foster home until a new home can be found for him. Do not be ashamed that you can no longer keep your dog. It is better to plan for his future than to have him put to sleep or left to wander the streets. Try to make a donation to the breed rescue fund for helping to find a new home for your family friend.

SELLING A DOG

Don't think for one moment a dog you bought for £1000 as a puppy will have gained value if you decide to sell him. It is so sad to see adverts for fully-grown dogs with a price tag attached. Your main concern should be that your dog finds a new home and is not a profit making exercise.

OLDER OWNERS

There will come a time when the owner may not be able to care for their dog. Can a family member step in and help, or perhaps a neighbour or friend? I know of elderly owners who, rather than be without a dog have a designated 'dogfather' who will take over the care of the dog if one day the owner is no longer able to.

There are canine dog charities that will take on your dog if you are old, infirm or terminally ill and can no longer care for him yourself. The Cinnamon Trust can step in and help you care for your dog or find a loving foster home for his remaining days. They never put a healthy dog to sleep and give your dog the love and care that he has been used to when living with you. Visit their website at: www.cinnamon.org.uk

Plan ahead for when you are no longer around to care for your dog. Mention him in your will and make sure that family knows what your wishes are with regard to your dog's future. Your dog's health and wellbeing should be considered at every stage of your life and his.

The author's thoughts

This chapter shows just what should be considered when owning a dog. They are not puppies for long and we have to face the future of dog ownership knowing what is in store for us as well as the dog.

11

Coping with bereavement

As our dogs grow older we must face the fact that they will
die. Even the best vets cannot keep them alive forever. We are
fortunate that if their pain becomes too much to bear or their
quality of life diminishes we can help them on their way. If your
dog is undergoing treatment your vet may recommend euthanasia,
but ultimately the choice is up to you. On the other hand your
dog may be quite happy at home but slowly the light bulb grows
dim and you realise that the dog you knew since his puppy days
is no longer there. It is the greatest kindness you can offer a dog
to release him from a life where he can no longer run through the
grass or sit in the sunshine. It is cruel to let him linger.

THE VET'S VISIT

Arrange for your vet to call to your home rather than take the
dog to the veterinary surgery. However frightened you are stay

with your dog and cuddle him as the vet inserts the needle into
your dog's leg. He will just fall asleep. It is not a nasty sight and
no different to him falling asleep at any other time. This time he
will not wake up.

Talk to your dog and tell him how much the family loved him. It
will help you cope and it doesn't hurt to cry either. Thanks to you
your dog had a wonderful life. Never blame yourself for calling
the vet; never question whether it was the right time to let him go.
Just remember your lovely friend and celebrate the wonderful life
you had together.

SPECIAL TREATS

I feel it helps to plan ahead for the last days of our dogs' lives.
Special treats, tasty meals and perhaps help them into the garden
or for a last drive in the car. Dogs are fortunate in that they have
no comprehension of the future or of death. Perhaps that is why
they cope with illness much better than us as they cannot fear
words they do not understand. Having owned a large number of
dogs I know exactly how I want my dogs' days to end: at home
if possible and with their siblings around them. The other dogs
need to see their brother, sister, aunt or uncle slip away. We have
lost four oldies in the past two years. Gracie did have to be put
to sleep when she was 13; her sister Peggy went peacefully in
her sleep at the grand age of 15. Brother William was almost 14
and had been ill for several weeks, but he was with my husband
at home. The last to pass away was Nelson (our Nellie) – he was
11 and a half and just fell at my feet. I thought he had tripped
and bent to help him but he rolled over, groaned and was gone.
Everyone told me it was a quick way to go. He had not been ill,

but I was devastated and horrified by the aggressive way he went. He was such a gentle, soft dog and it took a while for me not see his body writhing for the few seconds before he went every time I looked at the spot where he had died. In time I would smile to think that he died on the very spot where he had been conceived. He had been home bred and his mother and father had stood by the patio door as that mating took place.

PLANNING AHEAD

You do need to decide what to do with your dog's body after his death. It is better to plan ahead rather than make the decision on the day he passes away.

Home burial

This is probably the preferred place for your dog to rest. However, some people do not have gardens or may be planning to move home and do not like the idea of leaving their dog behind. If you do opt for a home burial dig the hole as deep as possible and once the dog is buried place several paving stones on top as, sadly, foxes will try to excavate the area. It is possible to purchase a coffin for your dog although these are not really needed for a home burial. You can find more information at www. dignitypetcrem.co.uk/

Removal by the vet

Your vet services will almost certainly include the disposal of your dog's remains. He will be taken with other dogs and cremated, then placed in a mass grave at the pet crematorium. This service is provided with the utmost respect and is used by many pet owners each year.

Pet cemetery

There are pet cemeteries throughout the UK where you can purchase a plot and have your dog buried. The grounds are beautiful places to visit and the headstones commemorating the lives of many much-loved pets will bring a tear to your eye. It is not unknown for the owners to have their own ashes scattered on their dog's grave when their time comes.

Cremation

It is possible to have your dog cremated and his ashes returned to you. Your vet will arrange this service for you and you will be notified when the ashes have been returned to the surgery. Some people like to scatter the ashes in a favourite area or to keep them in a special urn in the home. The choice is yours.

Personal service

Did you know that it is possible to take your dog to the crematorium and wait for the ashes? This is something that my husband and I do for each of our dogs. We attend the Cambridge animal crematorium and rather than wait for two to three hours we drive to a nearby garden centre and purchase a plant for our garden in remembrance of our dog.

Staff who are in attendance are very polite and the service provided is quite similar to when arranging funerals for adults. When a dog passes away at home your vet will be able to store him in a cool room for you if the crematorium is closed. We have often found that our dogs seem to pass away at the weekend or on a bank holiday and our vet has been very kind in offering help.

Prices and plans

When you have decided on your choice of send off make enquiries about procedures, opening times and prices and save them until they are needed. With my dogs in the twilight of their years I have a doggy funeral fund set aside so there is never any worry about finding money at a time of such distress.

The Association of Private Pet Cemeteries and Crematoria hold a list of reputable cemeteries, pet undertakers and crematoria and can help you make the right choice of service supplier in your area: www.appcc.org.uk/

BEREAVEMENT COUNSELLING

It is not unusual to feel an overwhelming grief when a pet has died. Trained counsellors are available to help us come to terms with our loss. The Dogs Trust, along with other pet charities and organisations can help at this sad time: www.dogstrust.org.uk/az/b/bereavement/bereavementhelpandcounselling

THE RAINBOW BRIDGE

For pet owners facing the loss of a pet the Rainbow Bridge has given much comfort. The author has never been known but to him or her we give our thanks. The Rainbow Bridge is where we all want to go to be reunited with our beloved pets when the time comes.

Just this side of heaven is a place called the Rainbow Bridge. When an animal dies that has been especially close to someone here, that pet goes to the Rainbow Bridge. There are meadows and hills for all of our special friends so they can run and play together. There is plenty of food, water and sunshine, and our friends are warm and comfortable.

All the animals that have been ill and old are restored to health and vigour. Those who were hurt or maimed are made whole and strong again, just as we remember them in our dreams of days and times gone by. The animals are happy and content, except for one small thing; they each miss someone very special to them, who had to be left behind.

They all run and play together, but the day comes when one suddenly stops and looks in the distance. His bright eyes are intent. His eager body quivers. Suddenly he begins to run from the group, flying over the green grass, his legs carrying him faster and faster.

You have been spotted, and when you and your special friend finally meet, you cling together in joyous reunion, never to be parted again. The happy kisses rain upon your face; your hands again caress the beloved head, and you look once more into the trusting eyes of your pet, so long gone from your life but never absent from your heart.

Then you cross the Rainbow Bridge together . . .

Author unknown

THE RESCUED DOG'S RAINBOW BRIDGE

Unlike most days at Rainbow Bridge, this day dawned cold and grey, damp as a swamp and as dismal as could be imagined. All the recent arrivals were confused and concerned. They had no idea what to think for they had never experienced a day like this before. But the animals that had spent some time waiting for their beloved people knew exactly what was happening and began to gather at the pathway leading to the Bridge to watch. They knew this was something special.

It wasn't too long before an elderly animal came into view; head hung heavy and low with tail dragging along the ground. The other animals on the pathway . . . the ones who had been at Rainbow Bridge for a while . . . knew the story of this sad creature immediately. They had seen it happen far too many times.

Although it was obvious the animal's heart was leaden and he was totally overcome with emotional pain and hurt, there was no sign of injury or any illness. Unlike the pets waiting at the Bridge, this dog had not been restored to his prime. He was full of neither health nor vigour. He approached slowly and painfully, watching all the pets that were by now watching him. He knew he was out of place here. This was no resting place for him. He felt instinctively that the sooner he could cross over, the happier he would be. But alas, as he came closer to the Bridge, his way was barred by the appearance of an Angel who spoke softly to the old dog and apologised sorrowfully, telling him that he would not be able to pass. Only those animals that were with their special people could pass over the Rainbow Bridge. And he had no special beloved people . . . not here at the Bridge or on Earth below.

With no place else to turn, the poor elderly dog looked toward the fields before the Bridge. There, in a separate area nearby, he spotted a group of other sad-eyed animals like himself . . . elderly and infirm. Unlike the pets waiting for their special people, these animals weren't playing, but simply lying on the green grass, forlornly and miserably staring out at the pathway leading to the Bridge. The recent arrival knew he had no choice but to join them. And so, he took his place among them, just watching the pathway and waiting.

One of the newest arrivals at the Bridge, who was waiting for his special people, could not understand what he had just witnessed and asked one of the pets who had been there for some time to explain it to him.

'That poor dog was a rescue, sent to the pound when his owner grew tired of him. The way you see him now, with greying fur and sad, cloudy eyes, was exactly the way he was when he was put into the kennels. He never, ever made it out and passed on only with the love and comfort that the kennel workers could give him as he left his miserable and unloved existence on Earth for good. Because he had no family or special person to give his love, he has nobody to escort him across the Bridge.'

The first animal thought about this for a minute and then asked, 'So what will happen now?'

As he was about to receive his answer, the clouds suddenly parted and the all-invasive gloom lifted. Coming toward the Bridge could be seen a single figure . . . a person who, on Earth, had seemed quite ordinary . . . a person who, just like the elderly dog, had just left Earth forever. This figure turned toward a group of the sad animals and extended outstretched palms. The sweetest sounds they had ever heard echoed gently above them and all were bathed in a pure and golden light. Instantly, each was young and healthy again, just as they had been in the prime of life.

From within the gathering of pets waiting for their special people, a group of animals emerged and moved toward the pathway. As they came close to the passing figure, each bowed low and each received a tender pat on the head or a scratch behind the ears. Their eyes grew even brighter as the figure softly murmured each name. Then, the newly-restored pets fell into line behind the figure and quietly followed this person to the Bridge, where they all crossed together.

The recent arrival that had been watching was amazed. 'What happened?'

'That was a rescuer,' came the answer. 'That person spent a lifetime trying to help pets of all kinds. The ones you saw bowing in respect were those who found new homes because of such unselfish work. They will cross when their families arrive. Those you saw restored were ones who never found

homes. *When a rescuer arrives, they are permitted to perform one, final act of rescue. They are allowed to escort those poor pets that couldn't find a place on Earth across the Rainbow Bridge. You see all animals are special to them . . . just as they are special to all animals.'*

'I think I like rescuers,' said the recent arrival.

'So does God,' was the reply.

Author Unknown

The author's thoughts

I seem to have been at the stage of saying goodbye to so many of my lovely dogs in the past few years. I do have a wonderful band of dog-owning friends and we grieve together as each of our dogs takes those first steps to the Rainbow Bridge. I can understand why so many people say, 'never again' when they lose a dog but given time another puppy will walk into their lives and be loved as much as their last dog.

Products For Puppies

Grooming, cleaning and disease control products
Animal Health Company
www.animal-health.co.uk/natural-canine-health-products.aspx

Goat milk for puppies
Top Life Formula
http://www.toplifeformula.com/

Thornits Ear Powder
www.petmeds.co.uk/p-528-thornit-ear-powder.aspx

Dog Poo Wormery
www.earth-essentials.co.uk/prod_details_dogwormery.htm

Veterinary Herbal Medicine
Dorwest Veterinary
www.dorwest.com

Dog coats
Equafleece
www.equafleece.co.uk

Cages and crates for home and the car
www.croftonline.co.uk

Canine seat belts
Company of Animals
www.companyofanimals.co.uk/products/muzzles-travel-and-visibility

Kong
Company of Animals
www.companyofanimals.co.uk/products/kong

Rugs and fleeces
Bronte Glen
www.bronteglen.co.uk

Natural nutritional supplements
Lintbells
www.lintbells.com

Laughing dog puppy meal
www.laughingdogfood.com/products

Butcher's Tripe
www.butcherspetcare.com

Mineral rocks for the water bowl
Dog rocks
www.dogrocks.co.uk

Books and Contact Information

BOOKS

Everest, E. (2010) *Canine Cuisine*. Oxford: How To Books Ltd.

Everest, E. (2009) *Showing Your Dog: a Beginner's Guide*. Oxford: How To Books Ltd.

Evans, J.M. and White, K. (1997) *Book of the Bitch*. London: Ringpress Books.

O'Driscoll, C. (1997) *What Vets don't tell you about Vaccines*. First Stone.

Billinghurst, I. (1998) *Grow your Pups with Bones*. Bathwurst, New South Wales: Ian Billinghurst.

Lonsdale, T. (2005) *Work Wonders: Feed your Dog Raw Meaty Bones*. Windsor, New South Wales: Rivetco Pty Ltd.

The Kennel Club (2003) *The Kennel Club Illustrated Breed Standards*. London: Ebury Press.

CANINE PUBLICATIONS

Our Dogs (weekly)
Subscriptions available
www.ourdogs.co.uk
Your Dog (monthly)
Subscriptions available
www.yourdog.co.uk

USEFUL CONTACTS

The Kennel Club
www.thekennelclub.org.uk
0844 463 3980

PDSA
www.pdsa.org.uk
0800 731 2502

Dogs Trust
www.dogstrust.org.uk
0207 837 0006

The Cinnamon Trust
www.cinnamon.org.uk
01736 757 900

Pets as Therapy
www.petsastherapy.org
01844 345 445

Guide Dogs
www.guidedogs.org.uk
0118 983 5555

My veterinary surgery (and one I would recommend)
Pilgrim Veterinary Clinic
London Road
West Kingdom
Kent
TN15 6EX
01474 852661
http://pilgrimspets.co.uk

Contributors

Thank you to the dog owners who have supplied comments for use in *A New Puppy in the Family*.

Sarah Alpe, Cambridge
Sarah lives in Cambridge with her two young daughters, Stephanie and Abbie. They are the proud owners of Freddie, a Cavalier King Charles Spaniel puppy. Freddie will be sharing family holidays and outings with the girls.

Kelly Rose Bradford, West London
Kelly Rose Bradford is a freelance journalist, broadcaster, mother and lapsed dog owner. Matilda, a West Highland White Terrier, is her first puppy in nearly 20 years, and like any new or returning doggy mum she's on a real learning curve! She hopes her new dog will mean lots more family fun for her and her son William, aged 8 (and a dropped dress size from all the walking!).

Terrie Cousins-Brown, Swansea
Terrie has been fortunate to be around dogs for all of her life being born into a family with Old English Sheepdogs. Her parents showed the dogs and she developed the same interest and began showing as a young girl. For the last 24 years she has owned Polish Lowland Sheepdogs (PONS), a highly intelligent and quite demanding breed. The PON is an excellent companion and friend for the family and a keen watchdog over his boundaries. She breeds the occasional litter of Polish

Lowlands – as this is a numerically small breed, breeders have a great responsibility to preserve the essence and character of the breed for future generations. She shows and judges and spends a considerable time exercising and grooming the dogs. They lead full and active lives enjoying the beach, cliffs and woods of the Gower countryside.

Catherine Burrows, North West Kent

Catherine is the mother of a young family living in North West Kent. She and her husband are looking into owning a Bulldog. They are registered with Bulldog breed rescue and have looked into both rescue as well as puppy ownership.

June and Barrie Crowe, Kent

June and Barrie have two rescue dogs. Cassie came from a nice home where it was discovered that a grandchild had an allergy to dog hair. Ellie came from Battersea at Brands and the Crowes are her third owners. She has separation anxiety problems and nervous aggression towards dogs she doesn't know. June said, 'Her separation anxiety is the hardest to live with as we know that if she is left she will get very distressed. We overcome this by having a dog-sitter. Never in our 40 years of dog ownership have we resorted to this before. However, once we take on a dog we never give up on them. We have had troublesome Greyhounds, naughty Lurchers and wandering Boxers and have loved them all.'

Hazel Davis, Linthwaite, West Yorkshire

Hazel Davis is a freelance journalist and lives with her partner Bob in West Yorkshire. Hank and Eric are both rescue dogs from the RSPCA. Hank is a Lurcher/Airedale cross (she thinks) and Eric is a Border Terrier.

Dawn Hudd, West Midlands

Dawn has owned dogs for most of her life. She also has cats and guinea pigs but has had rats, rabbits and birds – all cohabiting happily in the same house! At the present time her dog family consists of Cassie the Yorkie, Sadie the Springer and Fly the (95 per cent) Springer.

Anthony Milton, Cambridgeshire

Anthony has had Border Terriers for thirty five years. His first, Penny, came from Peebles in the Border country in December 1975, when Anthony and his wife lived in Aberdeenshire. Penny had several litters of puppies, and they have kept the line going, so that their latest puppy born in 2010 traces back to her. They lived in Aberdeenshire for over 20 years, and their Borders were brought up in the country. All their three children were brought up with Border Terriers, and they are greeted as friends when any of Anthony's seven grandchildren come to visit. He started showing Penny when she was about a year old, and has been showing ever since. Though they are show dogs they are primarily family pets and all live in the house. All their Borders are registered with the Kennel Club, and are named after single malt whiskies. Their kennel name is Baillieswells, which is where they lived in Aberdeenshire. Their present three are Baillieswells Caol Isla (pet name Solo), An Cnoc of Baillieswells (pet name Titch) and Baillieswells Isla (pet name Isla). As well as showing his Border Terriers, he also judges them at Championship level, including in Sweden. He has his own website: www.baillieswellsborderterriers.co.uk

Janet Swannell, Nottingham

Janet and her husband Davis bought their first Old English Sheepdog three months after they were married and have not been without one for the past 32 years. They have mourned the loss of a few old ones and although they tell themselves 'they will never put themselves through this again' they are grateful that they can still witness daily the joy and pleasure of watching Hugo and his mother, Josie, run through the woods. They don't think they could ever be without their dogs and have instructed their daughters that, should there be a dog or dogs around when they meet their demise their daughters will look after them. Their daughters did ask if they wouldn't mind having a Polish Lowland Sheepdog!

Anna Webb, London

Anna and her Miniature Bull Terrier, Molly, live in London. Anna tells her story: 'Molly came into my life after my father died as the first dog I owned as an adult. She immediately brought joy, endless fun and the chance to revisit my childhood, much of which was spent with dogs and at dog events, including Crufts. As a puppy Molly had to come everywhere with me. She was hard to train, being one of the most stubborn breeds with a mind of her own and strong opinions. But over the nine years we've built up a close bond, from TV and radio appearances through to being my co-pilot through the ups and downs of daily life. Although I've loved other dogs, Molly is the one that will tear my heart apart when that final day comes. She anticipates my every move, knows everything even when I'm calling from abroad and amazes her dog-sitter! The fact dogs aren't genetically programmed to live long enough, is the cruellest act of all.'

Index

Some other titles from How To Books

CANINE CUISINE
How to cook tasty meals and treats that your dog will enjoy

ELAINE EVEREST

The only way we can know that our beloved dog is getting a healthy and nutritionally balanced diet is if we prepare their food ourselves. In this book, Elaine Everest provides over 100 tasty and nutritional recipes for every occasion, from main meals cooked with organic ingredients to kibble and mixer biscuit substitutes and delicious biscuits and treats to supplement their diet.

There are even recipes for cakes that can be specially baked to celebrate birthdays and other fun occasions.

- Healthy treats that will keep dogs lean and fit
- Easy to prepare daily meals, even for the non-cooks amongst us.
- Easy to make training titbits, plus recipes to cook and freeze
- Cooling snacks for hot days
- Vegetarian meals, slimming meals and special diets for happy hounds.

With this handy book you'll never again need to purchase mass produced treats for your dog – and you'll save money too.

ISBN 978-1-84528-408-4

DOGGEREL
Moving memoirs of rescue dogs and their second lives, in poetry and prose

ANGELA PATMORE
Foreword by Joanna Lumley

Inside this book are the portraits and true stories of discarded dogs that were not afraid to love again. These wonderful characters, fifty out of over 100,000 dogs a year that are unwanted and abandoned by their owners in this dog-loving nation, have sad stories of abuse, neglect and dereliction to tell. But these lucky fifty have emerged triumphant and wagging, often against apparently insurmountable odds, to make their new owners very happy.

DOGGEREL is being sold in aid of the Association of Dogs' and Cats' Homes, which embraces many of the UK's animal charities large and small. Right now they need your help.

ISBN 978-1-905862-58-0